HOW JEWISH IS CHRISTIANITY?

TWO VIEWS ON

THE MESSIANIC MOVEMENT

Books in the Counterpoints Series

Are Miraculous Gifts for Today?
Five Views on Apologetics
Five Views on Law and Gospel
Five Views on Sanctification
Four Views on Eternal Security
Four Views on Hell
Four Views on Salvation in a Pluralistic World
Four Views on the Book of Revelation
How Jewish Is Christianity?
Show Them No Mercy
Three Views on Creation and Evolution
Three Views on the Millennium and Beyond
Three Views on the Rapture
Two Views on Women in Ministry

Stanley N. Gundry (S.T.D., Lutheran School of Theology at Chicago) is vice president and editor-in-chief at Zondervan. He graduated summa cum laude from both the Los Angeles Baptist College and Talbot Theological Seminary before receiving his M.S.T. degree from Union College, University of British Columbia, and his S.T.D. degree from Lutheran School of Theology at Chicago. With more than thirty-five years of teaching, pastoring, and publishing experience, he is the author of *Love Them In: The Proclamation Theology of D. L. Moody* and coauthor of *The NIV Harmony of the Gospels*.

HOW JEWISH IS CHRISTIANITY?

TWO VIEWS ON THE MESSIANIC MOVEMENT

William Varner

Arnold G. Fruchtenbaum

David H. Stern

John Fischer

Gershon Nerel

Louis Goldberg, general editor

Stanley N. Gundry, series editor

ZONDERVAN

How Jewish Is Christianity?

Requests for information should be addressed to:

Zondervan, *3900 Sparks Dr. SE, Grand Rapids, Michigan 49546*

Library of Congress Cataloging-in-Publication Data

How Jewish is Christianity? : two views on the Messianic movement / Louis Goldberg, general editor; contributors, John Fischer ... [et al.] – 1st ed.
p. cm. – (Counterpoints)
Includes bibliographical references and index.
ISBN 0-310-24490-0
1. Jewish Christians. I. Goldberg, Louis, 1923–2002. II. Fischer, John. III. Counterpoints (Grand Rapids, Mich.)
BR158.H677 2003
289.9–dc21 2003014649

Interior design: Nancy Wilson

Printed in the United States of America

CONTENTS

PREFACE

I came to Moody Bible Institute (Chicago, Illinois) in 1965 and spent thirty years on the faculty. My teaching in the area of Jewish studies put me in position to be able to carry out special research in which I studied a contextualized approach by new Jewish believers to declare who we are and how we may share our faith with others in our Jewish community. Already by 1969, the name of the Hebrew Christian Alliance became the Messianic Jewish Alliance. The Jewish youth of the counterculture years of the late 1960s and early 1970s wanted to see congregations structured with a more Jewish context. The appearance of an organization in the early 1970s called "Jews for Jesus" reminded Jewish people that, as Jews, we can and do accept Yeshua (Jesus) as Messiah and the atonement for our sin.

This was not exactly new, as this was the approach taken in Israel in the first century in the early church! But to the church of the twentieth century and to many pastors, it appeared radical. This was especially true for our friends among the missionary societies in the early 1970s. The reaction was swift. Many articles were written and messages delivered, indicating that somehow to introduce a Jewish context meant going back to the law—that Jewish believers were erecting a dividing wall, and therefore the outreach to Jewish people was going to be tainted. Finally, in the fall of 1976, I called for a weekend seminar at Moody Bible Institute where Messianic leaders, pastors, and mission leaders could gather together, share papers expressing each one's position, talk together over meals, and see if we could come to some consensus over this new expression.

I'm not sure we changed a lot of people's opinions, but at least we began talking to one another. A major issue facing first-century believers was what to do with Gentile peoples who wanted to be a part of this new body of the Messiah that was forming. Paul's letters and the council at Jerusalem (Acts 15) solved many of the problems, although by the end of the 400s a non-Jewish dimension was in effect, and many Jewish believers were practicing their faith in the same way as non-Jewish believers. Today, the problem is reversed: What should be done with Jewish believers who are a part of Messiah's body, the church, and want to have a culture that reflects their background but with a biblical base?

I am grateful that Zondervan desired to publish this book that reflects the views of five believers about how Messianic Jews can articulate and live out their faith. One contributor is a non-Jewish person and four are Messianic Jews. Most of us have known each other since the beginning of this new phase of the presence of Messianic Jews around 1970 and through subsequent years as our theological positions have coalesced into specific guidelines.

Two major views are considered. The first is presented by William Varner, a non-Jew, who articulates a powerful plea that we do not need the Messianic congregation. Jewish believers, according to Varner, can find all they need—in their beliefs and in their practice—in the church as it is presently structured. Dr. Varner (M.A. in Judaic Studies; M.Div.; Th.M.; Ed.D.) served as a pastor for seven years and dean of the Institute of Biblical Studies with Friends of Israel Gospel Ministry for seventeen years, and for the past seven years has served as professor of biblical studies at The Master's College, as well as the director of the Israel Bible Extension campus of this college in Israel. His books include *The Chariot of Israel: Exploits of Elijah; Jacob's Dozen: The Tribes of Israel;* and a soon-to-be-published volume on the Messianic prophecies.

Four contributors respond to Dr. Varner from diverging viewpoints. The first is John Fischer, who holds the Th.D. and Ph.D. degrees. He is the executive director of Menorah Ministries, founder of Congregation B'nai Maccabim in the Chicago area, founder and rabbi of Congregation Ohr Chadash, Clearwater, Florida, and professor and chairman of Judaic Studies and dean at St. Petersburg Theological Seminary, St. Petersburg, Florida. He has been involved in a number of positions with the Messianic Jewish Alliance and the Union of Messianic Jewish

Congregations. His books include *The Olive Tree Connection, Siddur for Messianic Jews,* and *Messianic Services for Festivals and Holy Days.* John has also written a number of articles in various publications.

The second response is by Arnold Fruchtenbaum (Th.M.; Ph.D.), who served with Chosen People Ministries and the Christian Jew Foundation in the past and now is director of his own work, Ariel Ministries. His books include *Israelology: The Missing Link in Systematic Theology; The Footsteps of the Messiah: A Study of the Sequence of Prophetic Events; Jesus Was a Jew; Hebrew Christianity: Its Theology, History and Philosophy; Biblical Lovemaking: A Study of the Song of Solomon; A Passover Haggadah for Jewish Believers; Messianic Christology;* and *Historical-Geographical Study Guide of Israel.* He has contributed articles for a number of books and other publications as well.

I am privileged to serve as the third respondent. After working as an engineer for seven years and coming to faith, I earned an M.A. in philosophy and a Th.D. I was a pastor for twelve years and was professor of theology and Old Testament at Temple Baptist Theological Seminary in Chattanooga, Tennessee for three years. I then served as professor of theology and Jewish studies at Moody Bible Institute in Chicago for thirty years. I served on the board of Jews for Jesus for nineteen years and for six and a half years on its staff as scholar-in-residence. I have written commentaries on Leviticus, Deuteronomy, Proverbs, and Ecclesiastes, as well as *Studies in Apologetics, Turbulence over the Middle East,* and *Our Jewish Friends.* I have also contributed articles and essays to a number of publications. I served on the Old Testament translation team for the New International Version and as a consultant on the Old Testament for the New King James Version. Between 1968 and 2000, I was privileged to spend entire summers in Israel visiting among the congregations.

The fourth respondent, Gershon Nerel, an Israeli, is a Jewish believer in Yeshua (as he would style himself). He holds an M.A. and a Ph.D. from Hebrew University. He has served as "Israel Secretary" for the International Messianic Jewish Alliance and has also been a member of the executive committee for the Messianic Jewish Alliance of Israel. He has written numerous articles on modern history, theology, sociology, and arts of Jewish believers in Yeshua in popular and scholarly journals. It is interesting that he and his wife and three of his brothers-in-law and their wives are members of Moshav Yad Hashmona, along with some Finnish brethren who founded the society just outside of Jerusalem. These believers have their own congregation and reach out to many Israelis. They follow the Mosaic covenant as much as possible; however, they do take careful note of what Yeshua did with this covenant and follow him accordingly. The oral law is assessed as totally outside of any consideration.

The second major view is that Messianic congregations surely do have a part within the body of the Messiah. But then a question immediately arises: How Jewish should these congregations be? Arnold Fruchtenbaum sets forth his view that Messianic congregations should indeed exist, but that they must not function contrary to the teaching of the New Testament. Once again, four respondents reply from their various viewpoints. These positions range from that taken by John Fischer, myself, and Gershon Nerel, who affirm the legitimacy of Messianic congregations but wrestle with how Jewish such a congregation can be, to that of William Varner, who does not admit the need for such a congregation.

A final essay in this book stands by itself in ascertaining the future of the Messianic witness through its congregations. Because David H. Stern wrote the insightful *Messianic Jewish Manifesto* in 1988, he is the most likely person to have a sense of where Messianic Judaism is headed in the future. I'm sure you will appreciate what he has to say.

Before David H. Stern became a believer, he already held a Ph.D. and was a professor at the University of California at Los Angeles. After he accepted Yeshua, he went on to earn an M.Div. degree. He was the translator of the *Jewish New Testament* from Greek to English, which serves to express the New Testament's Jewishness. His translation of the *Tanak* (Old Testament) is found, along with his New Testament translation, in the *Complete Jewish Bible.* He has also written the *Jewish New Testament Commentary* and *Restoring the Jewishness of the Gospel: A Message for Christians.*[1] In 1979 he, his wife, and their family made *aliyah,* or emigrated, to Israel, where they now live.

---

[1]These books are available from Jewish New Testament Publications, P.O. Box 615, Clarksville, MD 21029.

So there it is. We Jewish people have a saying: If we have two Jews in a debate, we can end up with three opinions! It just might be the same with non-Jewish believers, or there may be even more opinions when you read what we have written! I trust that the various views expressed in this book will be helpful as you work your way through the issues of what it means to have Messianic Jews remain in their own congregations yet work in harmony with the rest of the body of the Messiah.

LOUIS GOLDBERG, 1923–2002

Dr. Louis Goldberg, hailed as "a man of peace" by Jews for Jesus founder Moishe Rosen, died on October 22, 2002, just a few months after completing his work on this book. Dr. Goldberg came to faith in Yeshua as the Messiah in January 1948, and he left a lasting legacy of scholarship and faithful service. The contributors and publisher dedicate this book to Louis Goldberg in gratitude to God for his life and his legacy. "Precious in the sight of the LORD is the death of his saints" (Psalm 116:15).

INTRODUCTION: THE RISE, DISAPPEARANCE, AND RESURGENCE OF MESSIANIC CONGREGATIONS

Louis Goldberg

The response to Yeshua (Jesus) the Messiah among the Jewish community was numerically significant during two periods. The first occurred during the initial four hundred to five hundred years of the common era.[1] Yeshua's claim as the Messiah began the first response, and when the Spirit came upon the followers of the Messiah at *Shavuot* (Feast of Weeks; Pentecost), the *talmidim* (disciples) entered into a fruitful outreach. After these disciples passed on, other evangelists continued into the 300s. But when the professing church contextualized belief and practice into a Hellenistic context in the 300s to 400s, it had no room for Jewish seekers who wanted more of a Jewish religious cultural expression in their worship and lifestyle. This and other reasons led to the slim response between 500 and 1750, as will yet be noted.

However, by the 1750s to 1800s, many within the church had softened their approach to Jewish people, who then turned to accept Yeshua. The second fruitful response began by the end

---

[1]Parallel to world history, Jewish history is marked as Common Era and Before the Common Era.

of the nineteenth century, when a good number had become believers. The twentieth century saw even more. And now many Messianic congregations are present even in the land of Israel.[2]

THE GLORIOUS DAYS OF THE FIRST PERIOD

The First Century

Some figures of the number of believers are preserved in the New Testament. For example, we read about the three thousand (Acts 2:41), five thousand men (Acts 4:4), and many priests (Acts 6:7). Statements indicate that "the Lord added to their number" (Acts 2:47), "many who heard the message believed" (Acts 4:4), and "the number of disciples in Jerusalem increased rapidly" (Acts 6:7). After some twenty years, *Ya'akov* (James) and the elders told *Sha'ul* (Paul) of the thousands (literally "myriads" or "ten thousands") of believing Jews (Acts 21:20). In his letter to the Galatians, possibly written between 48 and 52, *Sha'ul* spoke of the congregations (churches) of Judea (Galatians 1:22).[3]

No other figures are available. When the Romans subdued Jerusalem in 70, the people of Judea suffered the loss of the second temple and the death of many people. The believers, however, loyal to what Yeshua had said concerning this disaster (Luke 21:20–24), before the fall of Jerusalem had fled to Pella, east of the Jordan River.

After A.D. 70 many Jewish believers in Yeshua returned to Jerusalem and found both leaders and people in utmost despair. How would they be able to worship God without the temple? But one of the leading religious leaders, Yohanan ben Zakkai, received permission from the Roman officials to have a study center for Jewish young people in the small community of Yavneh (Greek, *Jamnia*), not far from modern Tel Aviv. From 73

---

[2]Sponsored by the Caspari Center for Biblical and Jewish Studies in Jerusalem, a massive work is being undertaken by some of the finest scholars on the history of Jewish believers in Yeshua in three sections: antiquity (ca. 30–500), the Middle Ages (500–1700), and the present period (1700–present). When these volumes become available, they will add immeasurably to the knowledge we have of Messianic Jews across the centuries.

[3]James Montgomery Boice, *Galatians*, in The Expositor's Bible Commentary, vol. 10, ed. Frank E. Gaebelein (Grand Rapids: Zondervan, 1976), 420.

to 90, Yohanan, Gamaliel II, and many other religious leaders met on numerous occasions to restructure a Judaism without temple worship.[4]

So a spiritual vacuum existed in Judea between 70 and 100, and Jewish believers took advantage of the opportunity, but no written records remain of what was the response. Some have conjectured that 20 percent of the nation had accepted Yeshua by A.D. 100, but nothing tangible exists to support these assertions. Furthermore, the Council of Yavneh took steps to eliminate Jewish believers in the synagogues through the *Birkat HaMinim,* a derogatory statement directed against them.[5] The fact that this council singled out these believers suggests they may have wanted to create a barrier between themselves and the believers.

Did these Jewish believers have a distinctive name in the first century? Early Christianity scholar Ray Pritz affirms the term *Nazarenes,*[6] noting that Tertullus referred to *Sha'ul* (Paul) as the leader of these folks (Acts 24:5). If so, this derogatory term would have been well understood. Paul also defined believers as "followers of the Way" (Acts 22:4; 24:14).[7]

---

[4]This council of leaders became crucial in Jewish history, marking out what was to be the Hebrew Scriptures (Old Testament, or Written Law), excluding all other books, describing how atonement was attained without temple sacrifices, defining the structure of synagogue worship, as well as making a number of other decisions affecting the totality of Jewish life.

[5]Until A.D. 90, only individual synagogues put out Jewish believers from their midst, but Yavneh wanted them all out. By A.D. 80, a statement was added to the twelfth benediction of the *shemoneh esreh,* the morning prayer, "May all the *nozrim* [Nazarenes] and *minim* [heretics] perish in a moment." Genuine Jewish believers would have had a problem reciting this prayer, and overseers were present to see if any refused, which became the means to evict them, according to Ray A. Pritz (*Nazarene Jewish Christianity* [Jerusalem: Magnes Press, Hebrew University, 1992], 102–5).

[6]See Pritz, *Nazarene Jewish Christianity,* 13–14, who notes the "juxtaposition of the words *yishai* [Jesse] and *neser* [Branch]" in Isaiah 11:1 and also that Epiphanius suggested in the 300s that "the two names [Iessaean/Essene from Iessaios/Jesse—and Nazarene] were used before Christian."

[7]Pritz affirms this term to designate genuine believers from the first century, even though one does not see a general use of it until later in the 300s. Interestingly, the term today in modern Hebrew refers to non-Jewish believers while *Yehudim Meshihim* (Messianic Jews) describes Jewish believers.

The Second and Third Centuries

Ananus, the high priest, ordered *Ya'akov* (James, a brother of Yeshua) executed in 62,[8] and Simon, son of Cleopas, a cousin of Yeshua, became leader of the congregation until 107. At reportedly 120 years of age, he too was tortured and put to death—the last of Yeshua's family to hold this office.[9] Other Jewish believers held this post until 133.

The second revolt against Rome (132–135) proved even more disastrous than the first revolt (66–70). The Nazarenes wanted to fight, but another dilemma arose when Rabbi Akiva proclaimed the military leader, Simon ben Kosiba, to be *bar Kochba,* or "Son of the Star" (see Numbers 24:17), a conquering Messiah. The Nazarenes applied the passage only to Yeshua, so usage in any other way was considered blasphemy. Once again, the Nazarenes fled to Pella and other points east, and Jewish people never forgot or forgave this betrayal. Jewish believers in Israel today willingly fight in the Israel Defense Forces to prove their loyalty to the nation.

After A.D. 90, the designation of Jewish believers and beliefs became a question. In Justin Martyr's *Dialogue with Trypho* (ca. 132), the former complained that two beliefs existed in his day: Yeshua is human and preexistent with God, or he is only "a man of men."[10] Obviously, Justin could not agree with the second statement, which became the belief of the Ebionites. The designation "Ebionites" eventually became more and more the word used by non-Jewish believers to describe all Jewish believers. Origen (185–254) spoke similarly. Pritz points out that Origen's view was that one group of Jewish believers held to the humanity and deity of the Messiah, while the rest were faulted for their view of the Messiah's identity.[11] But the term "Ebionites" was

---

[8]See Paul L. Maier, *Eusebius, The Church History* (Grand Rapids: Kregel, 1999), 81–83 where Eusebius, citing Hegesippus in Book 5 of his *Memoirs,* carried the full account of James's horrific death.

[9]See Hugh J. Schonfield, *The History of Jewish Christianity* (London: Duckworth, 1936), 59–60.

[10]Justin Martyr, *Dialogue with Trypho,* cited in Pritz, *Nazarene Jewish Christianity,* 20–21.

[11]Origen, *Contra Celsum,* book 5, chapter 61, cited in Pritz, *Nazarene Jewish Christianity,* 21.

applied to all Nazarenes—a tactic to which Pritz would take exception.

Another Nazarene of the second century was the historian Hegesippus, born in Judea in 140. His writings were preserved by Eusebius (before 340).[12] He was one of the few Nazarenes who traveled widely in the Mediterranean world.

Few records remain of other leaders and patriarchs of the Nazarenes throughout the second century, although some of them must have been preserved by later writers. These include Hippolytus's *Refutation of All Heresies* (public ministry from 198 to 236) and the later Epiphanius's *Panarion* (or, also, a *Refutation of All Heresies*).[13] Congregations of these believers existed east of the Jordan River, in cities around the Sea of Galilee, in Syria proper, and east to modern Iraq—maintaining a witness to their people.[14]

The Fourth and Fifth Centuries

The fourth century is most crucial for the existence of the Nazarenes. Epiphanius was an important witness. Born in Judea in 315, he had a most prominent career, finally becoming bishop of Constantia (Salamis), indicating his ties with the non-Jewish church. In 382 he met Jerome in Rome, and they worked closely together.

The most devastating action against the Jewish believers was by non-Jewish believers, who contextualized faith and practice into the Greek-Roman culture. In the year 325 the emperor Constantine called a general council, and 318 bishops met in Nicea. But records indicate that at least eighteen bishops of Israel's interior were Jewish, yet the official lists only include those located in coastal cities and no Jewish bishops were invited.[15] Were these Jewish bishops completely unknown?

---

[12]See Schonfield, *The History of Jewish Christianity*, 95–96.

[13]See Pritz, *Nazarene Jewish Christianity*, 29.

[14]Schonfield, *The History of Jewish Christianity*, 90, citing *Panarion*, xxxix, 7 and xxx, 18.

[15]Bellarmino Bagatti, *The Church from the Circumcision* (Jerusalem: Franciscan Printing Press, 1971), 86–87.

Or did Constantine and the non-Jewish bishops intentionally avoid any Jewish presence at all? Could the decisions of Nicea have been different had Jewish believers been present?

The council drew up a statement concerning the deity of Yeshua cast in a Greek philosophical frame of thinking, yet reflecting biblical truth. But Nazarenes also held to this basic truth, although they set it in a Jewish framework to best communicate it to their people. The observance of Easter was another issue. The Nazarenes observed Passover on 14 Nisan and also remembered then the death, burial, and resurrection of Yeshua. Non-Jewish believers wanted to observe the resurrection of Jesus from their view, calculated on a slightly different basis from that of Passover: Good Friday was the day of Yeshua's death and the Sunday afterward the day of his resurrection. Still another question was worship on *Shabbat* (Sabbath) versus Sunday. Most bishops preferred worship on the first day of the week, and so the council at Nicea decided for the latter.

This council enforced these decisions as the *only way* to understand theology and practice. While the council at Jerusalem (Acts 15) granted a certain amount of freedom of choice to the non-Jewish believers in their beliefs, worship, and lifestyle, at Nicea none was granted to the Nazarenes. If Jewish believers had insisted on their contextualized testimony, they would have be regarded as heretics by the non-Jewish church. Bellarmino Bagatti's comment on this tragedy was that the "divergence did not touch the substantial doctrines of Christianity, but it did have enough influence to bring about a great division of souls."[16]

Jewish people became the target of strong dislike and even hatred, as seen in Constantine's letter of anti-Jewish sentiments[17] and Chrysostom's anti-Jewishness in eight homilies in

---

[16]Ibid., 93.

[17]Eusebius, "On the Keeping of Easter," *Vita Const., Lib.* iii, 18–20, cited by Philip Schaff and Henry Wace, eds., *Nicene and Post-Nicene Fathers*, vol. 14 (New York: Scribner's Sons, 1900), 405.

the year 386.[18] The Christian law codes of emperors Theodosius I (379–395) and Theodosius II (408–450) caused Jewish people to suffer legal, political, and social ostracism; so while their lives were spared, the rulings made of Jewish people second- or third-class citizens.[19] The Nazarenes began to diminish greatly during the fifth and sixth centuries,[20] and with their demise non-Jewish believers lost a part of the natural bridge to Jewish people. Even though the Messianic Jewish presence had almost disappeared, it would not be forgotten by future generations of Jewish believers.

THE SECOND PERIOD: CONVERSIONS TO THE CHURCH

This second period of Jewish history and the presence of Jewish believers in the Messiah makes for dismal reading. Once the expression of faith by non-Jewish believers of this period became the official religion, Christendom also took on a political power that would be difficult to substantiate from a New Covenant theology.

Until the 1500s

The Crusades are a record of atrocities during the twelfth century: the slaughter of Jewish people, Arab Muslims, and Arab Christians. Early in the thirteenth century, England, France, and Germany expelled their Jewish populations. In 1492, when the last of the Muslims left Spain, King Ferdinand and Queen Isabella also ordered out the Jewish population, except for Jewish people who would convert to Christianity. Beginning in the 1500s in Italy, and spreading to most European countries, Jewish people were forced to live in ghettos, apart from the rest of

[18]See Paul Johnson, *A History of the Jews* (New York: Harper & Row, 1987), 165.

[19]See Edward H. Flannery, *The Anguish of the Jews* (New York: Paulist, 1985), 55–58.

[20]Jerome often met with these people in the fifth century, knew them well, and even translated their gospel of Matthew into Latin; Pritz, *Nazarene Jewish Christianity*, 50–53.

the population. At least a hundred thousand Jews were slaughtered in the Ukraine from 1648 to 1658.[21]

When a Jewish person in Europe believed in Yeshua, he or she had to renounce all ties with Judaism and accept wholeheartedly an identity with Christianity in all its facets. Only in this way could church leaders be sure of a complete break with the rabbis' teachings. Such a person renounced his Jewish name and was given a "Christian" name.

From the sixth century on, the record of Jewish believers in Yeshua is a list of only a few individuals, except for unusual circumstances in Spain. At times, sincere Jewish believers sought to share with their people in a soft, appealing manner, but the non-Jewish clergy supporting the Jewish believers only made matters worse by then resorting to heavy-handed methods of forcing Jews to choose between conversion and death.

An interesting record relates to the Spanish period prior to the Muslim invasion in the early 700s. Beginning in 589, all Jewish people faced forced conversions, and over a hundred thousand became "Christians." Surprisingly, Julian, the son of one of the converts, demonstrated a genuine interest, eventually becoming an outstanding archbishop by 680. He spoke kindly to Jewish people, appealing to them to find the true way to salvation. In the eastern part of the empire, disputations occurred between Jewish and Christian leaders, and some Jewish people were convinced that Yeshua is the Messiah.[22]

In 711 Spain was conquered by the Muslim armies, and, interestingly, Arab Muslim leaders used Jewish people in different levels of government. The pressure on Jewish people lessened, and on occasion some Western monarchs sat in on disputations between Jewish and Christian scholars.

In one such case, a Moses Sephardi was baptized in 1106 in Aragon, territory recaptured by the Spaniards. Named Petrus Alfonsi, he became the physician to the king and also a well-known writer. In a final work, he wrote lovingly to Jewish people, seeking to encourage them to believe in Yeshua the Messiah, using biblical prophecy.[23]

---

[21]See Johnson, *A History of the Jews*, 259–60.

[22]See Schonfield, *The History of Jewish Christianity*, 135.

[23]Ibid., 140.

Nicholas Donin was a freethinker in Paris whom the rabbis excommunicated. After ten years of separation, he became a believer; and then in 1238, with the authority of the church and pope behind him, he ordered copies of the Talmud destroyed.

Some twenty-five years later in France, Pablo Christiani became a believer and rose in the ranks of the Dominican order. He debated with Rabbi Nachmanides before King James I of Aragon concerning the claims of Yeshua, attempting to prove from the Talmud, especially the *haggadah* (narrative) passages, that Christianity is true and that the Messiah is both God and man.[24] The rabbi argued well, stating that he did not believe all the *haggadah* accounts himself, but the Dominicans claimed the victory. Even though Jewish people suffered some distress, yet there appeared to be an appreciation by Christians of the depth of Jewish thought and practice.

Abner of Burgos (1270–1348), another Jewish believer, made a profound impression on the Jewish communities through his many writings in both Hebrew and Spanish. Two other Jewish believers, one of whom was John of Valladolid, disputed in the 1300s with Moses Ha-Cohen over the claims of Yeshua. Sixty-nine sessions over a twenty-one-month period (1413–14), supported by the Jewish Christian Andreas Baltram, later bishop of Barcelona, were held between a number of rabbis and Geronimo de Santa Fe (formerly Joshua ben Joseph). In the end, five thousand Jewish folks made the decision to accept Yeshua![25]

Solomon HaLevi (1351–1435), as rabbi of Burgos, was encouraged to read the Messianic prophecies of the *Tanak*, especially Jeremiah 31. He came to faith and took the name Pablo de Santa Maria. His two brothers were also baptized, but his wife delayed her decision. He became archbishop of Burgos, and many Jewish people believed, including his mother and eventually his wife. Four sons were also believers; two were high churchmen, the third was a recognized man of letters, and the fourth was a soldier.

Jewish people heard the Word in the Mediterranean world during this period: in Italy from the cleric Anacletus II (who died

---

[24]See Johnson, *A History of the Jews*, 218–20.

[25]See Schonfield, *The History of Jewish Christianity*, 151.

in 1138), and also from Gregory, a Jewish physician in the Middle East, who became a primate in the Eastern church in 1266.

A "converts' home" was located in England, and even though many Jewish people were expelled, enough remained that some became believers and needed a place to reside. Eventually two homes existed, one in Oxford and one in London, lasting until the 1800s, and several hundred Jewish folks lived there across the years. One Jewish Christian, Nicholas de Lyra, had to leave England because of the banishment of Jews by Edward I in 1290. Educated in Oxford, he found a home with the Franciscans in Paris and was baptized in 1291. He eventually taught theology until 1325. He had a good grasp of hermeneutics, and his most impressive work was a commentary on Scripture, explaining the *Tanak* and New Covenant on what he judged to be correct principles. Martin Luther and others likewise were greatly affected by this work. Likewise, many other writings of Jewish believers had an impact on the Catholic Church as well as on the Reformation.

Again, the church authorities in Spain stirred up the multitudes against the Jewish people in their key cities from 1390 until the mid-1400s. At least fifty thousand Jewish people were massacred, while the baptized numbered into the hundreds of thousands. Possibly some thirty thousand were genuine, and many mounted the ranks of the church hierarchy. All the others who were forced to be baptized kept only an outward form of being faithful to the church. Many were then arrested and tortured by those who ran the inquisition; but even with their confessions, some were put to death anyway.

Finally, in early 1492, the last of the Muslims were driven from Spanish soil. By March of that year, Jewish people were faced with the edict of expulsion. They had four months to leave Spain, but those who converted could stay. Most left, and five years later the same edict was enacted in Portugal.

Throughout the 1500s to the Early 1700s

Two movements significantly influenced the religious and intellectual life in Europe: the Renaissance and the Reformation. While a conspicuous change in attitude did not occur immediately among the Protestants toward Jewish people, eventually some attitudes began to change. Protestants took seriously the Hebrew language and literature because of their keen interest in what the Scriptures had to say. The renaissance of an optimistic humanism[26] considered people as human beings, even the Jewish person! Both movements eventually led to the emancipation of Jewish people.

The numbers of Jewish Christians during the 1500s to 1750 were increasing all the more and one can find them teaching in well-known universities all over Europe. Jewish believers were present in all branches of the church, not only among Protestants but also among Catholics and Greek Orthodox.

THE THIRD PERIOD (1750 TO THE PRESENT): AN INFLUX OF JEWISH BELIEVERS

From the 1750s to the present day, Jewish believers have grown steadily in number, particularly during the twentieth century. We hardly have the space to describe the great numbers of individuals, except to refer to the societies or organizations working among Jewish people.

The great missionary awakening in the Protestant church during the latter 1700s and the early 1800s stirred many to the need to reach out to Jewish people in a more humane manner of sharing the message. With societies in England, Scotland, and Germany, emissaries went all over Europe and were met with fruitful response, as Aaron Bernstein noted in a number of different examples.[27] The nineteenth century saw at least 250,000 Jewish people come to faith, according to existing records of various societies.

In addition, because of the Zionist awakening and the response of both religious and secular Jews to move back to the

---

[26]At least in an optimistic humanism man is considered to have value and dignity, even though it is self-assigned. Man can therefore be involved in creativity in many areas; see Roger E. Olson, *The Story of Christian Theology* (Downer's Grove, Ill.: InterVarsity Press, 1999), 349. Humanism becomes destructive when man is considered to have no value, but only a mere machine to be used by the state.

[27]Aaron Bernstein, *Jewish Witnesses for Christ* (Jerusalem: Keren Ahvah, 1999, first published in 1909). A treasure is provided in the biographies of many of these people, as well as in the books each one wrote.

homeland, English and Scottish medical doctors, nurses, teachers, and special emissaries also went to the land of Israel during the 1800s, establishing hospitals, churches, schools, and a number of preaching points. In one instance, response also occurred through the Anglican Church in Jerusalem and the consecration of its first Jewish bishop, Michael Alexander, who saw at least thirty-one Jewish people turn to the Lord in the four years (1841–45) of his ministry.[28]

The testimony expanded in various ways and places. In 1866 in Great Britain, a number of Jewish believers came together to form the Hebrew Christian Alliance. The founders of the alliance were members of churches, but the issue of Jewish congregations did not die. God led Joseph Rabinowitz[29] in the last decade of the 1800s to reach out to his people; and Rabinowitz then started new congregations, calling this movement "Israelites of the New Covenant."[30] He was baptized in Berlin and then invited to join the Lutheran and the Russian churches, but he refused. No doubt he had his problems with the established church because of the new Messianic congregations he had started, but the point was that Jewish believers did not forget what was a distinctive Jewish witness in the beginning. While Rabinowitz died in 1899, the work continued until the beginning of World War I in 1914. Some attempt was made after that conflict to keep the work going.

Since then, an international Hebrew Christian Alliance was also founded in 1925, representing organizations of Jewish believers in principal countries in Europe, North and South America, South Africa, and Australia, as well as in Israel. Within a short period, articles about several issues appeared in the magazine of the alliance—*The Hebrew Christian*—as well as letters and statements of faith for Hebrew Christian congregations, indicating again that the presence of congregations of Jewish believers was never forgotten.

---

[28]See Bernstein, *Jewish Witnesses for Christ*, 77–90.

[29]Not much is known as to how Rabinowitz came to the Lord, but it must have occurred during his visit to Israel. God definitely spoke to his heart, first leading him to faith and then commissioning him to return to the Ukraine to begin a new work among Jewish people.

[30]See Schonfield, *The History of Jewish Christianity*, 225.

The organization (now the International Messianic Jewish Alliance) has an international meeting about every fifth year, and it is most heartening to see Jewish believers attend from all over the world.

The next movement was a ministry to reach Jewish people in the United States through the efforts of David and Esther Bronstein in Chicago. But the reception of these new Jewish believers in a number of Presbyterian churches was not the best, and an outreach worker from one of the churches encouraged the Bronsteins to start a Jewish church.[31] The first Hebrew Christian congregation began in 1934 in Chicago and soon others came into existence in Oak Park, Michigan; Philadelphia, Pennsylvania; and Newark, New Jersey. These congregations were not as fully into the Jewish religious culture as many Messianic congregations are today, but they retained just enough of the background to remind these believers where they came from.

The Hebrew Christian churches had less of an attraction by the 1960s, although by the early 1970s another wave of Jewish people became believers. For the most part, these young folks wanted to be more in touch with the roots of their grandparents. As a result, Messianic congregations came into existence that, more or less, contextualized the religious culture of Jewish people. While the attempt was to carefully guard the experience with a sound understanding of the Word of God in general and the teachings of Yeshua in particular, sometimes it has worked and sometimes not enough safeguarding has been maintained to protect what the *Tanak* (Hebrew Scriptures, or Old Testament) and New Covenant teach.

The result today is that there are more than three hundred Messianic congregations in the United States, while some ninety Messianic congregations exist in Israel. And the number of Messianic Jewish people keeps growing all the while. Most of us who are Jewish believers see ourselves as here to stay. We are the natural bridge to our people. Every effort is being taken to train young people for future ministry among Jewish people or

[31]See Janet Hoover Thoma, ed., *Esther* (Elgin, Ill.: David C. Cook, 1980), 158. The emissary told the Bronsteins that if Swedish peoples have their congregations, then why raise the question if Jewish believers should have their own as well?

to lead Messianic congregations, Messianic music continues to grow, and almost every Jewish person knows of the presence of Messianic Jews. The number of Jewish believers today almost rivals what was present in the first century—a wonderful testimony to the special work of the Spirit of God that has brought us to this point in our history.

The history of Jewish believers is a fascinating one, but life for Messianic Jews has been difficult ever since the Greek contextualization of the Christian message and lifestyle. Jewish believers had to conform to this lifestyle, giving up their identity and culture to become non-Jews as they joined the church. Should it be any wonder, when thinking back to the situation of the first century, that Jewish believers want a context that is Jewish? Obviously, the Judaism of the first century is not what it is today, but just the idea that Yeshua and the early disciples lived in a Jewish context is enough to attract many Jewish believers to want to live and function in this kind of context today, as long as biblical principles are maintained.

I trust the pros and cons expressed by the writers in this book will enable you to see the issues concerning the place and function of Jewish believers more clearly. I hope that somewhere amidst all the viewpoints, you, the reader, will recognize that these believers do have a vital role to play—not only in terms of reaching their own people in their own culture context, but also as those who serve the entire body of the Messiah.

Chapter One

MESSIANIC CONGREGATIONS ARE NOT NECESSARY

William Varner

MESSIANIC CONGREGATIONS ARE NOT NECESSARY

William Varner

Anyone writing about Messianic Judaism is faced with serious challenges. Not the least of these is what exactly to call the movement. The term "Messianic" could refer to any Jewish person who believes in a personal Messiah, whether or not that Messiah is identified with Jesus of Nazareth. For example, the Lubavitcher Hasidim[1] fervently proclaim their belief in "Moshiach" (Messiah), some even to the point of identifying their former "Rebbe" (Rabbi Schneerson) with that Moshiach. Does that mean that Lubavitchers are also "Messianic Jews"?

Nevertheless, the term "Messianic Judaism" is here to stay, so it is fruitless to argue about its semantic nuances. This chapter will use the term, even though many may not believe it to be the best title. Likewise some within the movement prefer "congregation" over "synagogue" to describe their local body of believers. Recognizing this diversity of expression, I will simply use "Messianic synagogue" for convenience. Messianic Judaism, whatever the strengths or shortcomings of the title may be, is a fait accompli—and it is that which we will attempt

[1]Lubavitchers are a group of Hasidic Jews based primarily in the Crown Heights area of Brooklyn, New York. Ultra-Orthodox in their Judaism, Lubavitchers desire to evangelize other Jews with a view to bringing secular and liberal Jews back into the fold. The name *Lubavitch* refers to a town in Lithuania that was the center of the movement during the nineteenth century.

to evaluate in the light of theological, historical, and pragmatic considerations.

The movement, in its modern form, is now about thirty years old. This book, therefore, is probably a quarter of a century late. Most of those in Messianic Judaism have made up their minds by now and will probably not be dissuaded by any arguments that I propose against their position. On the other hand, readers interested in exploring the questions Messianic congregations inevitably raise may find some help here as they sort out those issues.

Consider another obstacle we face in evaluating the movement. Which form of Messianic Judaism am I addressing? In the early 1990s a Reconstructionist rabbi named Carol Harris-Shapiro made an ethnographic study of Messianic Judaism.[2] Ethnography involves the researcher entering a community as both an observer and, to an extent, a participant. While other full-length treatments of Messianic Judaism have been done by non-Messianic Jewish writers,[3] Harris-Shapiro's work is a fairly reliable treatment by someone who, as an outsider, tried to view the movement from the inside. She summarizes the various organizational strands of Messianic Judaism into five basic groups:

1. Union of Messianic Jewish Congregations
2. International Alliance of Messianic Congregations and Synagogues
3. Fellowship of Messianic Congregations
4. Association of Torah-Observant Messianics
5. The International Federation of Messianic Jews

Referring to the last three as the smaller of the five, Harris-Shapiro adds, "These Messianic margins point to the increasing diversity in the movement, while their small numbers highlight the strength of the mainstream expression of Messianic Judaism."[4]

---

[2]Carol Harris-Shapiro, *Messianic Judaism* (Boston: Beacon Press, 1999).

[3]David Rausch, *Messianic Judaism: Its History, Theology, and Polity* (Lewiston, N.Y.: Edwin Mellen, 1982); and B. Z. Sobel, *Hebrew Christianity: The Thirteenth Tribe* (New York: John Wiley & Sons, 1974).

[4]Harris-Shapiro, *Messianic Judaism*, 28–29.

Therefore, to whom do my observations apply? I will leave this question to be answered by the reader, who must realize that I paint with a broad brush. If I wrongly cover someone, I fully realize that such is inevitable in light of the movement's great diversity.

Before I address my concerns, I would like to share a few personal observations about myself and my interest in this subject. First, I rejoice greatly in the fact that God is preserving a remnant of Jewish believers, as Paul would say, "at the present time" (Romans 11:5). Jewish evangelism has always been a major factor in my life, even after seminary during my seven years as a pastor. I then had the privilege of working with a ministry to Jewish people for seventeen years, ten of which I served as dean of a Bible institute dedicated to teaching students, many of whom were Jewish believers, about the history and culture of the Jewish people both in America and Israel. I received a master's degree in Judaic Studies under the tutelage of a well-known Conservative Rabbinical scholar and gave the valedictory address at graduation in a Philadelphia synagogue. Recently my teaching has been primarily to Gentile Christian students and it has been a joy to introduce them to the culture, history, and spiritual need of the Jewish people. In this teaching connection, I am also the director of our college's branch campus program in Israel and have led thirty-six study trips to that country. There I have tried to familiarize myself with the challenges that "Yehudim Meshichim" (Messianic Jews) face in their homeland.

I write this, not to impress anyone, but to let the reader know that, although I am a Gentile, I write as one who is a sympathetic friend to Jewish believers. One of my ministry goals has always been to educate the churches where I minister about the Jewish people and about Israel and to expose anti-Jewishness wherever it raises its ugly head. So let my criticisms of Messianic Judaism be understood in this light. If I wound anyone, be assured that it is done in the spirit of the proverb: "Faithful are the wounds of a friend . . ." (Proverbs 27:6 NASB).

A VOICE FROM THE PAST

Jewish Christianity is certainly not a modern phenomenon, but has existed since the first century. As an identifiable movement within the church, however, it ceased to exist by the sixth century A.D.[5] A renaissance came during the nineteenth century, when literally thousands of Jewish people came to faith in Jesus as Messiah. Jewish Christian organizations formed, and new Jewish missions appeared in England, in America, and on the Continent. Some of the greatest "giants" in Jewish Christianity lived and ministered in the late nineteenth and early twentieth centuries. Among the most notable was the great David Baron, who came to faith in Jesus from an Orthodox European background and went on to found the Hebrew Christian Testimony to Israel in England. Baron contributed major scholarly works that are still read and appreciated today, such as *Rays of Messiah's Glory; Types, Psalms and Prophecies; Israel in the Plan of God*; and the invaluable commentary, *Visions and Prophecies of Zechariah.* The editor of this current volume has written, "Many of David Baron's friends testified that he was the most Christlike man they had ever known."[6]

Most of Baron's writing originally appeared in the periodical *The Scattered Nation,* the magazine of the "Testimony." In 1911 he published an article in that periodical titled "Messianic Judaism; or Judaising Christianity." Reading this article should remind us of the statement made by Qohelet (the Teacher) in Ecclesiastes that "there is nothing new under the sun" (Ecclesiastes 1:9). This article makes it clear that the Messianic Jewish movement is not a new phenomenon but was significant enough at the turn of the last century to cause great concern to David Baron. The concerns he expressed ninety years ago should be noted today, especially since he was such a highly regarded Jewish believer.

Baron writes that the movement's founders, such as Theodore Lucky, advocated

> that it is incumbent on the Hebrew Christian not only to identify themselves with their unbelieving Jewish brethren in their national aspirations—as explained, for instance, in Zionism ... but to observe the national rites and customs of the Jews, such as the keeping of the

[5]See Hugh J. Schonfield, *The History of Jewish Christianity* (London: Duckworth, 1936), chapter IX.

[6]Louis Goldberg, *Our Jewish Friends* (Neptune, N.J.: Loizeaux, 1983), 167.

> Sabbath, circumcision, and other observances, some of which have not even their origin in the law of Moses, but are part of the unbearable yoke which was laid on the neck of our people by the Rabbis.[7]

Baron cites writers who prepared both a "Minimum Programme" and a "Maximum Programme" for their turn-of-the-century form of Messianic Judaism. The "Minimum Programme" advocated the following:

> A Hebrew Christian movement will hold fast to Passover, Pentecost, Tabernacles, Chanucah, and Purim; will include in its liturgy a good deal of the traditional Synagogue prayer; will be favorably disposed towards every ceremony that has entwined itself in the Hebrew consciousness; . . . insists on circumcision; attaches itself to the Hebrew consciousness and holds by the historical and Biblical continuity of Israel's mission.[8]

This was the "Minimum Programme." In Baron's words, the "Maximum Programme" also included "joining in all forms and ceremonies of the Christ-rejecting synagogue, to wear phylacteries and the talith, to use the Jewish liturgy, just as the other Jews do, only to smuggle in now and then the Name of Jesus into their prayers."[9]

Baron also mentions the following in a section he calls the "Dangers of the Movement":

> These Judaizing brethren forget that during the period of Israel's national unbelief a *new thing* is being formed. Every essential element of what constitutes *nationality* is to be found in this new brotherhood. Those who profess allegiance to Christ become members of the body of which He is the Head, and must be ready to take up the cross and follow Him. And one very heavy part of the cross is the separation which it involves to disciples . . . from those near and dear to them. It is hard to bear suffering and reproach, but the conditions of discipleship are

---

[7]David Baron, "Messianic Judaism," *The Scattered Nation* (October 1911): 4. Reprinted by American Messianic Fellowship (Chicago, Illinois).

[8]Ibid., 4.

[9]Ibid., 4.

not different now than they ever were. "He that taketh not his cross and followeth after me is not worthy of me."[10]

Baron then compares the present situation of the Jewish believer to the scene in Exodus when "anyone inquiring of the LORD would go to the tent of meeting outside the camp" (Exodus 33:7): "So also during this much longer period of national apostasy God's tabernacle is removed from the camp of corporate official Judaism, and everyone from among Israel who in truth seeks the Lord must be prepared to go forth unto Him [outside] the camp, bearing His reproach."[11]

Lastly, Baron stresses the unity of Jews and Gentiles in the terms of Galatians 3:28 ("neither Jew nor Greek") and the picture of unity in one body found in Ephesians 2:11–22.

> Now, to say that in the one Church of Christ are one set of rules, one attitude in relation to certain rites and observances enjoined in the law, and certain earthly or "ritual hopes" and expectations are incumbent on its Jewish members, which are not incumbent on its Gentile members, is nothing less than to try to raise up again the middle wall of partition which Christ by His death hath broken down, and to introduce confusion into the one "House of the Living God." The New Testament nowhere tells the Gentile believer that he is "free" from anything from which the Jewish believer is not freed.[12]

Baron concludes this section by offering that Paul also had in mind Jewish as well as Gentile believers in his strong warning against law keeping in Galatians 4 and 5.[13]

I mention one more significant point that Baron makes, since it lays the groundwork for one of my own points to be expressed later. He mentions the claim that is often made by advocates of Messianic Judaism that the early Jewish believers remained in unbroken continuity with the Hebrew nation and attended the temple and synagogue worship and kept the Sabbath and the Jewish festivals, as is evident in the Acts of

---

[10]Ibid., 6.
[11]Ibid., 7.
[12]Ibid., 8.
[13]Ibid., 8.

the Apostles. He deals with this issue by declaring that it was the unbelieving synagogue that made this "unbroken continuity" between church and synagogue an impossibility by driving the Nazarenes from their midst. "What these brethren overlook is that in relation to this and other matters the Acts of Apostles introduces us to a transition period and describes conditions which most evidently were not intended by God to be permanent."[14]

Baron's point is that the destruction of the temple should have ended once and for all any perplexity that the Hebrew Christian may have had about what were called those "national observances." "With the breaking up of the Jewish national polity there emerged the Church of Christ—not dependent upon any building or land for its center of unity, and whose worship does not consist in observances but in spiritual sacrifices and service which are acceptable to God through Christ Jesus."[15]

I have summarized Baron's article to illustrate that Messianic Jewish issues were alive well over a century ago—and also were strongly opposed by one of Hebrew Christianity's greatest lights. For the rest of this chapter, I would like to build on what Baron so passionately wrote out of concern for his fellow Jewish believers and for the overall cause of the Messiah.

BIBLICAL-THEOLOGICAL CONCERNS

Concerns expressed about the Messianic Jewish movement have been largely theological in nature. To these biblical-theological issues I would like to add some historical and pragmatic concerns. While the first area could be considered the most important, the historical and pragmatic areas also raise significant concerns about Messianic Judaism and Messianic synagogues.

Three general propositions will serve to summarize the first area of my biblical-theological concerns. The fourth point expresses what is only a potential theological danger at this present time.

---

[14]Ibid., 13.

[15]Ibid., 13.

1. The apostle Paul described his previous life in "Judaism" as something that was part of his past life, *not something that was part of his present life.* The only occurrences of the word "Judaism" in Paul's speeches in Acts or in his New Testament epistles are in Galatians:

> For you have heard of my previous way of life in *Judaism*, how intensely I persecuted the church of God and tried to destroy it. I was advancing in *Judaism* beyond many Jews of my own age and was extremely zealous for the traditions of my fathers.
>
> GALATIANS 1:13–14, emphasis added

The context of this passage clearly indicates that those practices that were part of Paul's "Judaism" ended when God revealed his Son in him (1:15–16). This "Damascus Road experience" in Acts 9 so completely reoriented Paul's thinking that he never afterward identified with "Judaism" as a way of life. Why, therefore, would some Jewish believers desire to be part of any form of "Judaism"?

This does not mean that Paul thought he had ceased to be a Jew. He makes this clear in many places, both in Acts and in his epistles (Acts 22:3; Romans 11:1). But his involvement in "Judaism" ended when Jesus was revealed in him. He was then part of something new. How, then, can modern Messianic Jews desire to take part in the rituals of their pre-Messiah life?

Paul uses even stronger language in Philippians about that past life:

> If anyone else thinks he has reasons to put confidence in the flesh, I have more: circumcised on the eighth day, of the people of Israel, of the tribe of Benjamin, a Hebrew of Hebrews; in regard to the law, a Pharisee; as for zeal, persecuting the church; as for legalistic righteousness, faultless.
>
> But whatever was to my profit I now consider loss for the sake of Christ. What is more, I consider everything a loss compared to the surpassing greatness of knowing Christ Jesus

my Lord, for whose sake I have lost all things.
I consider them rubbish, that I may gain
Christ.

PHILIPPIANS 3:4–8

In listing the privileges and attainments of his life prior to knowing the Messiah, Paul first grouped together privileges that were his by birth and could never be changed (circumcision, membership in Israel and Benjamin, and his Hebrew-speaking heritage). The second set of attainments were those things he accomplished by his own effort (Pharisaic membership, persecuting zeal, and his Torah-observant life). He did not view these things, however, as badges of honor but rather as impediments to pleasing God. He describes them with a very strong word—"rubbish." Although he had lost all of these human attainments, he had no regrets. Knowing Jesus as his Messiah was far more valuable than any of these privileges and accomplishments.

This does not mean that Paul became an example of the "self-hating Jew" described in so much of the recent Jewish literature. It means that those practices that some Messianic Jews emphasize so strongly are the very things that can often lead to self-righteousness and actual loss of the real knowledge of the Messiah. While many today want to find their identity in "Jewishness," Paul found his identity in the Messiah.

I know these are strong words, but Paul's words are even stronger than mine. The usual response to this is to point out the incidents in Acts where Paul observed certain Jewish rituals such as the Nazirite vow (Acts 18:18; 21:23–26). These incidents, however, cannot be interpreted to contradict his clear teaching in Galatians and Philippians, as well as what will be seen in Ephesians and Colossians. Paul's actions, however, should be viewed as illustrating *personal* choices rather than exemplifying a pattern of congregational worship. His actions have been "overinterpreted" to justify a pattern of observance they were never intended to exemplify.

Furthermore, the absence today of the temple with its elaborate ritual is a serious factor that needs to be taken into sober consideration. How does the lack of the temple impact the observance of these and other ritual practices that belong to another time and often cannot be observed today in the way they were originally commanded? A more serious question also arises: Where in the New Testament record can it be shown that the ritual practices of Second Temple Judaism ever characterized the congregational pattern of the early churches?

2. *Messianic Judaism tends to promote divisions that the redemptive work of Jesus has torn down.* The key texts in this regard are Ephesians 2:11–22 and Galatians 3:28. I will not quote the entire Ephesians passage. It should be evident that it clearly proclaims the spiritual unity of all Gentile and Jewish believers in one body. I would like to focus on two verses in chapter 2:

> For he is our peace, who has made us both one, and has broken down the dividing wall of hostility, by abolishing in his flesh the law of commandments and ordinances, that he might create in himself one new man in place of the two, so making peace.
>
> EPHESIANS 2:14–15 RSV

Most interpreters believe that this text must be interpreted with the layout of the Herodian temple as its background. Paul declares that the work of the Messiah has resulted in his abolishing the "law of commandments and ordinances" (the Greek text reads literally "commandments *in* ordinances"). At the very least this would refer to the disannulling of the ceremonial laws and also the so-called "civil laws" of Exodus 21–24. The exact Greek phrase "law of commandments" is in the Greek Septuagint translation of Exodus 24:12, referring to what God had given to Moses on the mount up to that point.

Paul further illustrates this unifying work of the Savior by referring to the fence (*soreg* in Hebrew) that kept Gentiles from entering the sacred area of the temple (*naos* in Greek) where only Jews could enter and worship. This dividing wall, in the Pauline spiritual analogy, has been abolished because that which kept us apart—the "law of commandments"—has been disannulled. Both believing Jews and Gentiles can now enter together, not into some physical temple, but into something brand-new: the body of the Messiah.

It has sometimes been charged that Messianic Judaism is rebuilding this dividing wall of hostility. Actually, no one can rebuild the wall. It is done away with forever. My concern, however, is that Messianic Judaism, by its emphasis on laws that have no continuing spiritual relevance for either Jews or Gentiles, is creating an appearance that the wall still separates us.

A prominent Messianic Jewish commentary on the New Testament spends pages trying to explain these verses as not referring to the Mosaic laws at all. The commentary states that the "ordinances" referred to in Ephesians 2:15 are not the laws of Exodus but are the *takkanot*—rabbinic ordinances added to the Torah, such as the one pertaining to the dividing wall.[16] This bifurcation of "commandments" and "ordinances" with the idea that the Messiah abolished the latter and not the former cannot be sustained by any fair reading of the text. It also smacks of special pleading, i.e., avoiding the plain reading of the text due to a preconceived position. No other commentary I have consulted makes this imagined distinction between divine and human commands in this text. Charles Hodge is representative of the scholarly consensus on this passage:

> This may mean the law of commandments *with* ordinances—referring to the two classes of laws, moral and positive; or it may refer to the form *in which* the precepts are presented in the law ... *tōn entolōn* giving the contents of the law, and *en dogmasin* the form.[17]

The most authoritative Greek lexicon does not support the idea that the "ordinances" are rabbinic decrees, but defines them as the specific ordinances in which the commandments are expressed.[18] The author of the previously cited Messianic commentary confuses the issue greatly by calling these ordinances *takkanot*. This is a rather anachronistic comment, however, since these rabbinic decrees refer almost exclusively to much later decisions, such as the *takkanah* banning polygamy

---

[16]David H. Stern, *Jewish New Testament Commentary* (Clarksville, Md.: Jewish NT Publications, 1999), 588.

[17]Charles Hodge, *Commentary on the Epistle to the Ephesians* (Grand Rapids: Eerdmans, 1966), 134.

[18]F. W. Danker, ed., *Greek-English Lexicon of the New Testament*, 3d ed. (Chicago: University of Chicago Press, 2000), 254.

in the eleventh century A.D.[19] The article on *takkanot* in the *Encyclopedia Judaica* nowhere refers to the fence in the temple as an example of a *takkanah*.[20]

I have taken extra space in this section to illustrate the lengths to which some proponents of Messianic Judaism will go to explain away texts that clearly teach that observance of Jewish ordinances confounds the unity that Jewish and Gentile believers share in their Messiah.

One of the key texts in this entire discussion is Galatians 3:28: "There is neither Jew nor Greek, slave nor free, male nor female, for you are all one in Christ Jesus." The three pairs of people mentioned in this verse focus on ethnic (Jew/Gentile), social (slave/free), and gender (male/female) distinctions. It is obvious that such distinctions do not just disappear when we come to the Lord. To say that no one can speak of himself as a Jew or a Gentile anymore is foolish, for then one could not speak of himself as a free man, a slave, a man, or a woman! Paul addresses all of these groups by name in his epistles (e.g., Colossians 3:18–4:1).

It is clear that the unity described is a spiritual one. But how we manifest this unity in congregational life is the crucial question. If it is necessary to establish Jewish congregations to accommodate Jewish believers, is it necessary to establish slave congregations or female congregations to also meet their needs? Do not the epistles indicate that the early churches had all these groups in them, each finding their needs met in the Messiah and not in ceremonial observances or cultural identity? If we seek to establish such congregations, are we not running contrary to the whole emphasis of Galatians 3:28? Ought we not to seek the ideal of congregations that exemplify the unity of the body so that all ethnic, social, and gender differences matter nothing in the spiritual unity of the body? Shouldn't we pattern our worship in such a way as to flesh out what it means to be "all one in Christ Jesus"? Shouldn't we urge our congregants to seek their identity in their Lord and not in their culture?

---

[19]Jacob Neusner, editor in chief, *Dictionary of Judaism in the Biblical Period* (Peabody, Mass.: Hendrickson, 1999), 614.

[20]"Takkanot," *Encyclopedia Judaica*, CD-ROM edition (Jerusalem: Judaica Multimedia, 1997).

3. *Messianic Judaism emphasizes the "shadow" of Old Testament typical, or symbolic, practices when we should be emphasizing the "reality" of New Testament fulfillments.* The key text here is Colossians 2:16–17 (but Galatians 4 and Hebrews 10 also affirm what this passage teaches):

> Therefore let no one pass judgment on you in questions of food and drink, or with regard to a festival or a new moon or a Sabbath. These are only a shadow of what is to come; but the substance belongs to Christ.
>
> COLOSSIANS 2:16–17 RSV

Paul states that two main categories of the Mosaic law—dietary restrictions and festival observances—as important as they were to the Old Testament Israelite, were intended to be temporary from the very beginning. They were only shadows, cast by the Messiah backward in time. Now that we have the "substance" (the reality, the fulfillment of the type), why would anyone encourage others to continue to practice the shadow? F. F. Bruce wrote the following:

> Under the Levitical economy the observance of such days, like the food laws, was obligatory on the Jews. But now the Christian has been freed from obligations of this kind. If a Christian wishes to restrict himself in matters of food and drink, or to set apart days for special observance or commemoration, good and well.... But to regard them as matters of religious obligation is a retrograde step for Christians to take.[21]

The stress on these observances in many Messianic circles certainly leaves the impression that they are viewed "as matters of religious obligation."

Some defenders of Messianic Judaism have argued that Paul is addressing only Gentiles here and that the words simply do not apply to Jewish believers. This also is the case, according to some, when Paul so strongly opposes the observance of time-bound

[21]F. F. Bruce, *Commentary on the Epistle to the Colossians* (Grand Rapids: Eerdmans, 1957), 244.

festivals: "You are observing special days and months and seasons and years! I fear for you, that somehow I have wasted my efforts on you" (Galatians 4:10–11).[22] Suffice it to say, however, that no one can prove that the Colossian and Galatian churches were completely or even predominantly Gentile. Scholarly commentaries provide abundant evidence of large Jewish communities in the Lycus Valley location of Colosse.[23] While it is true that the Colossian heresy was a mixture of Jewish and Gnostic ideas, there were plenty of Jewish elements in it to argue for a Jewish presence in the church. Why would these Jewish believers be exempt from this warning? Furthermore, J. B. Lightfoot provides extensive evidence for a large Jewish population in the region of Galatia during the first century A.D. and also demonstrates that there were significant numbers of Jewish believers in the Galatian church.[24]

Paul nowhere indicates in either of these two epistles that he is addressing Gentile believers only and omitting Jewish believers in these warnings. If it is wrong for Gentiles to follow shadows, it is wrong for Jews as well!

Such a supposed disjunction in the apostolic teaching regarding the "shadows" (i.e., these warnings apply to Gentiles and not Jews) is certainly answered by a consideration of the epistle to the Hebrews. "For since the law has but a shadow of the good things to come instead of the true form of these realities, it can never, by the same sacrifices which are continually offered year after year, make perfect those who draw near" (Hebrews 10:1 RSV).

This one verse is only a small part of the much larger word of exhortation found in this book written primarily to Jewish believers. If there is any place where defenders of Messianic Judaism should find support, it should be in this document, but just the opposite is the case. The anonymous author states that as good as were the prophets and the angels and Moses and the ceremonial law, Jesus is better! After a careful consideration of Hebrews 8–10, it is hard to conclude otherwise than that the

---

[22]See Stern, *Jewish New Testament Commentary*, 611, 558.

[23]See Bruce, *Commentary on the Epistle to the Colossians*, 244.

[24]J. B. Lightfoot, *Epistle of St. Paul to the Galatians* (Grand Rapids: Zondervan, 1957), 9–10, 26–27.

institutions of the Mosaic law have been replaced by something far better—the reality of which they were only the shadows! Therefore, why would anyone want to confuse believers by emphasizing ephemeral observances when we have the reality of which the observance was only a shadow? To use these "shadows" as wonderful teaching tools is well and good; to use them as worship ordinances in our congregations is attempting to reverse redemptive history.

So much more needs to be said about the implications of this epistle for our study. May I simply remind the reader of the last of the author's famous "hortatory subjunctives": "Let us, then, go to him outside the camp, bearing the disgrace he bore" (Hebrews 13:13). All believers, Jewish or Gentile, are called to suffer outside the camp of whatever religious system they were in previously. Jesus did not please the Jewish religious leaders of his day, and he suffered because of it. Messianic Jews will never be able to please Jewish religious leaders today, no matter how "Jewish" they try to be. They must be willing to suffer because of this fact. Therefore, I urge all my readers to join Jesus outside the camp of rabbinic "Judaism," which is actually the Judaism of the last nineteen centuries. His company will sweeten any suffering you may endure.

4. My last concern, which may or may not develop into a major problem, is this: *I have noticed a tendency in a few Messianic writers to raise the issue of Jesus' deity in ways that seek to redefine this subject for Jewish believers.* The reason given is that the Trinitarian discussions of the fourth century were framed in Greek philosophical terminology rather than in Jewish categories. I do appreciate the desire to frame these truths in ways in which Jesus and the New Testament writers expressed them. I am concerned, however, about this tendency because one wonders how it will develop.

In the early centuries, some Nazarenes slipped into a heresy called Ebionism, which affirmed Jesus' messiahship but denied his deity. Attempts to redefine the doctrines so carefully hammered out at Nicea and Chalcedon make me nervous. Will this effort result in limiting the full deity of Messiah? What purpose will be served, since any teaching affirming that Jesus is more than human will still be rejected by Judaism? What appears to be a desire to express truths in a less "Greek" way may actually be encouraging an unintended slide toward Ebionism. All I can say at this point in time is *caveat lector* ("let the reader beware!").

HISTORICAL AND PRAGMATIC CONCERNS

Having traced four areas of theological concerns, I now will briefly discuss a few historical and pragmatic concerns I have about Messianic Judaism.

1. *Messianic Judaism must face the reality that it is simply impossible to return to the same situation that Jewish believers faced in apostolic times.* Many of the arguments advanced by Messianic Jewish authors seek to recreate for today the conditions that existed before A.D. 70. That is simply impossible, and therefore unwise. Three historical events must be factored into this discussion:

- the destruction of the temple in 70.
- the decisions at Yavneh around 80.
- the Simon bar Kochba aftermath in 132–135.

The first event ended Jewish believers' possible participation in temple observances, something that can clearly be found in the book of Acts (e.g., 3:1; 21:26). Early church historians mention that the Nazarenes even fled to Pella before the war and returned afterward.[25] It must have been a sobering experience for them to recall their Master's prophetic words recorded in Matthew 24:2. If we believe that the destruction was determined by God, we simply cannot utilize arguments from Acts that are tied to that system. Furthermore, since so many ceremonial observances were intimately involved with the temple ritual, how can we emphasize their observance today, especially in their modified rabbinical form? The current observances of Shavuot and Yom Kippur, for example, differ radically from their Old Testament observances and are given entirely different interpretations by the rabbis.

In the post-destruction decade, the Pharisees, under the leadership of Yohanan ben Zakkai, reorganized Judaism along Pharisaic lines at Yavneh (Greek, *Jamnia*). One of the many decisions made there was the introduction into the *shemoneh esreh*

[25]See Eusebius, *Ecclesiastical History III*, 5.

(morning prayer) of the much-discussed *Birkat HaMinim*, which was basically a curse pronounced on the Nazarenes and heretics.[26] This innovation made it impossible for Jewish believers to continue participating in the synagogue worship. In other words, Yavneh finally ejected Jewish believers from participation in the synagogue. Most Messianic Jews today do not attempt to continue worshiping in nonbelieving synagogues. This momentous event, however, should impact any idea that somehow the synagogue will accept Jewish believers. Attempts to contextualize Messianic synagogues to make them more acceptable to modern Jews simply ignore the events at Yavneh.

The Nazarenes could not support Simon bar Kochba's rebellion in 132–135 due to Rabbi Akiva's advocacy of him as Messiah. Although the sources are scanty, it appears that this pseudo-messiah strongly persecuted the Nazarenes.[27] This effectively led to their final rejection even from the Jewish community in addition to their earlier expulsion from the synagogue.

Faith in the messiahship of Jesus is consistent with the Hebrew Scriptures. Such faith, however, was declared clearly and finally to be inconsistent with "Judaism" in the aftermath of the generations following A.D. 70. To attempt to remain part of "Judaism" or even the Jewish community is to ignore these historical realities and is an anachronistic action. The parting of the ways between synagogue and church clearly took place by the year 135. Nothing said by the rabbis in nineteen centuries since has even begun to reverse these events.

However we may disagree with their decisions, the Jewish community does have the right to define who belongs to that community. However they may be inconsistent with Scripture and even with later rabbinical rulings about "who is a Jew?" they do have the right to be inconsistent and wrong. Therefore, as painful as it may be to some, Jewish believers today are not part of that Jewish community. Like Paul they need to realize that their identity is not to be found in their Jewishness but in their Savior: "And in [Christ] you have been made complete" (Colossians 2:10a NASB).

---

[26]See Jacob Jocz, *The Jewish People and Jesus Christ* (Grand Rapids: Baker, 1979), 51–57.

[27]Jocz, *The Jewish People and Jesus Christ*, 71.

2. *The idea that Messianic synagogues are a more effective witness to the Jewish community ignores historical realities.* There are no hard statistics to prove this idea and the fact remains that many Jewish people coming to faith in Jesus still find their spiritual home in Bible-teaching churches. All aspects of the body have benefited by the increased harvest of Jewish believers in the last thirty years. There is nothing more than anecdotal evidence to show that Messianic synagogues are more effective witnesses to Jewish friends and coworkers than are godly believers who are members of churches. Many of the members of these Messianic congregations are actually transfers from churches.

Another historical reality is that most members of Messianic synagogues were led to the Lord by Gentile believers. Even most of the Messianic leaders today were led to the Lord by Gentile believers or grew up in Jewish believing homes not involved in the movement. It is strange that some who argue that Messianic synagogues are more effective in Jewish evangelism were actually evangelized by Gentiles.

Historically, some current advocates of Messianic Judaism originally opposed these "new" ideas. The American Board of Missions to the Jews, now called Chosen People Ministries, issued a statement against the movement in 1976.[28] Consider also the conclusions of another early opponent of establishing separate congregations for Jewish believers:

> The main problem with a Hebrew Christian church, however, is that it goes against the biblical ideal of Gentile and Jewish believers worshiping and functioning together in the local church.... Establishing Hebrew Christian churches is not the solution to the problem.... Such a solution robs the local church of the benefits it can derive from having Hebrew Christian members.... The local church must be composed where possible of both Jewish and Gentile believers working together for the cause of Christ.[29]

What happened to cause these and other leaders to change their positions?

---

[28] Daniel Fuchs, "Messianic Synagogues," *The Chosen People* (January 1976): 14.

[29] Arnold Fruchtenbaum, *Hebrew Christianity: Its Theology, History, and Philosophy* (Grand Rapids: Baker, 1974), 94, 96.

3. *By taking Jewish believers away from good churches, Messianic Judaism is actually contributing to the greater "Gentilization" of the church.* Thus, the legitimate complaint that the church is "too Gentile" becomes worse the more the exodus takes place. We need each other in the body. Gentile believers need their Jewish brethren—not in some theoretical way, but in tangible ways—to remind them of the Jewish roots and Hebraic contours of our shared faith. Jewish believers also need their Gentile brethren to keep them from possible ethnocentricity, a potential danger for any ethnic group, not just for the Jewish people!

4. *The more Messianic synagogues that develop, the more the church is relieved of its mission obligation to reach out to the Jewish people in evangelism and discipleship.* It has always been difficult to get the church to see its duty to embrace the factor of "first for the Jew" (Romans 1:16) in its mission program. If Messianic synagogues become the norm, an attitude of "defer and refer" will become the attitude of the church. Churches will think that they simply cannot reach Jewish people and will "defer" that responsibility to Messianic synagogues, to which they can then "refer" them. This is clearly an unbiblical attitude and a denial of the Great Commission. Churches need to be challenged with their obligation to provide a place where Jewish people can be welcomed and can hear the gospel. If Messianic synagogues are the only place where this can happen, then the church is relieved of that sacred responsibility.

5. *By emphasizing so many nonbiblical Jewish observances, Messianic Judaism falls under Jesus' condemnation of the oral law of the Pharisees.* Practices such as wearing the yarmulke and the tallit as a separate garment, specific ways in which many holidays are observed, as well as the Bar/Bat Mitzvah celebrations, have no basis in the Torah but date from rabbinic and sometimes even medieval times. The danger of adding to the Word of God, even unwittingly, needs to be seriously considered in light of Jesus' warning about the "traditions of men" (Mark 7:8; see Matthew 15:3–9). All churches have traditions, but the problem arises when we make these traditions part of the worship ordinances and give the impression that they are what God desires us to do. Immature believers do not always have the discernment to distinguish between preferences and commands. Unfortunately, many Messianic synagogues give the impression that God

expects these things—even when they were added in later centuries by the rabbis.

A CONCLUDING MODEL

Many churches have failed to minister the Good News in a Jewishly sensitive way. Insensitive anti-Jewish comments often abound. Churches desperately need to rediscover the Jewish roots of their faith. All these are valid criticisms. I personally do not believe, however, that Messianic Judaism and Messianic synagogues are the answers to these concerns. Yes, it will take time, but don't give up on the church. The church won't improve its Jewish sensitivity if Jewish believers abandon it. Consider also an alternative to Messianic synagogues utilized for generations—a Hebrew Christian fellowship within a church:

> The solution is not to organize separate Hebrew Christian churches, thus violating the biblical norm, but to organize Hebrew Christian fellowships where believing Jews can come together as often as they like. Such a fellowship would help to meet the needs of new believers, hold children's classes in Jewish studies, and become a center for Jews to reach out to unbelieving Jews, and be a place where Hebrew Christians can gather to study the Scriptures in a Jewish context and perform the functions involved in the various Jewish celebrations.[30]

Many of these Hebrew Christian fellowships are still active in churches today.

I do not believe, therefore, that Messianic Judaism and Messianic synagogues have a biblical-theological, historical, or pragmatic justification. I am sure there can be exceptions in extraordinary circumstances, such as some situations in Israel. This chapter, however, does not deal with exceptional situations but with more normative concerns.

In conclusion, let me urge my readers to look at a specific church in the New Testament as a model to emulate. That church was not in Jerusalem but in Antioch of Syria (Acts 11:19–26). It was really there that the "church," in its multicultural and

---

[30]Fruchtenbaum, *Hebrew Christianity*, 97.

multiethnic dimensions, was truly born. Antioch cannot simply be explained away as a "Gentile church," because it is evident from the context that Jews were already being reached there when Gentiles also began to come to the Lord in great numbers. A potentially explosive situation in a mixed Jewish-Gentile congregation was channeled into peaceful paths by the wisdom of the encourager, Barnabas, and the exhorter, Saul (Paul). It was also in this church that Peter's inconsistent Jewish behavior was later rebuked by Paul (Galatians 2:11–14), rescuing the church from legalistic disaster.

Let us then try to follow the example of the church at Antioch. We need congregations like Antioch that flesh out the truth of Galatians 3:28. We need congregations like Antioch that do not just say "Gentiles are welcome" but proclaim a Messiah who is for *all* men and women. We need congregations like Antioch where the center of their fellowship is not culture but Christ. Finally, let us also remember that it was in Antioch where we all were first called "Christians."

YES, WE DO NEED MESSIANIC CONGREGATIONS!

A Response to William Varner

John Fischer

In pointing out that there is a problem with the very term "Messianic" when describing Jews who have affirmed Jesus (Yeshua) as Messiah, Varner is correct. Many Jews who would not acknowledge Yeshua do consider themselves Messianic as well. In addition, numbers of people who have affiliated with Messianic synagogues feel somewhat ill at ease with the adoption of this term by Jewish followers of Jesus who remain outside the Messianic congregational movement. Yet, while the term is less than precise, as William Varner points out, "(it) is here to stay." Recognizing these caveats, this response will use the term to describe those Jews who have accepted Yeshua as their Messiah *and* affiliate themselves with Messianic synagogues.

While Varner utilizes the ethnographic treatment of Messianic Judaism by Rabbi Carol Harris-Shapiro[1] as the basis of his assessment, he appears to be unaware of similar descriptive studies, such as those of Rabbi Dan Cohn-Sherbok,[2] Dr.

[1]Carol Harris-Shapiro, *Messianic Judaism* (Boston: Beacon Press, 1999).

[2]Dan Cohn-Sherbok, *Messianic Judaism* (London: Cassell, 2000); idem, ed., *Voices of Messianic Judaism* (Baltimore, Md.: Lederer, 2001).

Shoshanah Feher,[3] or Dr. Jeffrey Wasserman.[4] Each of these contributes significantly to the understanding and analysis of this rather diverse movement, a diversity that Varner rightly notes. As such, they, too, deserve to be consulted as part of the consideration and assessment of the Messianic synagogue movement. It is also intriguing to note that these authors acknowledge that Messianic Judaism *is* a legitimate part of the larger religious Jewish community, and, additionally, they urge the broader Jewish community to recognize Messianic Jews as part of the community.

A VOICE FROM THE PAST

As part of this discussion, it is important to note, as Varner has done, that Jewish belief in Yeshua is by no means a modern phenomenon. It existed through the first several centuries, quite likely into the seventh century, as the archaeological remains of Capernaum seem to indicate.[5] And it was a viable, vital movement that retained its connections to the larger Jewish community, as evidenced by some of the patristic literature.[6] Closer to this century, there was the reemergence of Jewish faith in Yeshua, numbering approximately a quarter of a million people in various strategic locations throughout Europe and England in the late nineteenth and early twentieth centuries.[7]

While for some, like Varner, David Baron is the name that stands out during this latter period, for others, men like Joseph Rabinowitz, Isaac Lichtenstein, and Paul P. Levertoff are the more

---

[3]Shoshanah Feher, *Passing Over Easter: Constructing the Boundaries of Messianic Judaism* (Walnut Creek, Calif.: AltaMira, 1998).

[4]Jeffrey Wasserman, *Messianic Congregations* (New York: University Press of America, 2000).

[5]Eric Meyers, "Early Judaism and Christianity in the Light of Archaeology," *Biblical Archaeologist* 51 (June 1988): 76.

[6]For example, Epiphanius, *Panarion* xxxix, 7; xx, 6:7–9; Jerome, *Letter to Augustine*.

[7]See Louis Goldberg, *The Task Before Us*, a paper delivered at the Consultation on the Variations of Life and Expression of Jewish Believers (Moody Bible Institute, Chicago [18–19 November 1977]).

significant figures.[8] They were leaders in an earlier "Messianic congregational" movement. So to exhaustively cite Baron, thus implying that he had some special merit or impact because he was a Jewish believer and noted writer—and is somehow determinant for Messianic theology then and now—implicitly denigrates these other Messianic Jewish pioneers. While it may be helpful to Varner's argument to use Baron, he is by no means the only capable, scholarly Jewish believing voice from the past that could and should be cited. For example, Lichtenstein wrote presciently and pointedly this response to a special emissary from the pope:

> I will remain among my own nation. I love Christ. I believe in the New Testament, but I am not drawn to join Christendom; so I will remain among my own brethren, as a watchman from within and to plead with them to behold in Jesus the true glory of Israel.[9]

Lichtenstein's position is thoroughly in keeping with that of Theodore Lucky and others, as cited by Varner (pages 32–33). And their positions, in turn, match the historical descriptions of the Nazarenes, the earliest Messianic Jews, as noted by the fourth-century church leader and historian Epiphanius:

> They are mainly Jews and nothing else. They make use not only of the New Testament but they also use the Old Testament of the Jews; for they do not forbid the books of the Law, the Prophets, and the Writings.... They practice circumcision, persevere in the observance of those customs which are enjoined by the Law, and are so Judaic in their mode of life that they even adore Jerusalem as if it were the house of God ... so that they are approved by the Jews from whom the Nazarenes do not differ in anything, and they profess all the dogmas pertaining to the prescriptions of the Law and to the customs of the Jews, except they believe in Christ.... They preach that there is one God, and his son Jesus Christ. But they are very learned in the Hebrew language; for they, like the Jews, read the whole

[8]See the testimonies from famous rabbis who came to faith, in John During, ed., "Special Rabbis' Edition," *Good News Magazine* (Johannesburg: n.d.); Kai Kjaer-Hansen, *Joseph Rabinowitz and the Messianic Movement* (Grand Rapids: Eerdmans, 1995).

[9]During, "Special Rabbis' Edition," *Good News Magazine*, 40.

> Law, then the Prophets.... They differ from the Jews because they believe in Christ, and from the Christians in that they are to this day bound to the Jewish rites, such as circumcision, the Sabbath, and other ceremonies.[10]

And these Nazarenes merely followed in the footsteps of their forebears, the apostles, about whom the second-century church father Irenaeus noted, "They themselves continued in the ancient observances.... Thus did the apostles scrupulously observe the dispensation of the Mosaic law."[11] So the modern Messianic Jewish movement has excellent historical precedents it is following.

Another problem arises with the use of David Baron's critique of Messianic Judaism. A subtle suggestion underlies its use, namely, that Baron's criticisms have not been answered. In reality, as Varner should be aware, the very criticisms Baron raises have already been addressed, and have been addressed repeatedly, by numerous authors over quite a number of years.[12] In other words, Baron's objections are "old news," and they *have* been answered "of old."

Baron—and Varner—apparently have a problem with "the historical and Biblical continuity of Israel's mission" (page 33). They would rather stress the "separation" and "new thing"—in other words, the discontinuity the gospel apparently brings. This is not a critique specific to Messianic Judaism but is merely part of a larger, ongoing theological discussion.[13] And, the Baron-Varner position ignores clear areas of major continuity expressed

---

[10]Epiphanius, *Panarion* xxxix, 7.

[11]Irenaeus, *Against Heresies*, 1.26.

[12]Some of these responses include: Philip Goble, *Everything You Need to Grow a Messianic Synagogue* (Pasadena, Calif.: William Carey, 1974); Daniel Juster, *Growing to Maturity* (Gaithersburg, Md.: Union of Messianic Jewish Congregations, 1982); Michael Schiffman, *The Remnant* (Baltimore, Md.: Lederer, 1989); David H. Stern, *Messianic Jewish Manifesto* (Jerusalem: Jewish New Testament Publications, 1988); idem, *Restoring the Jewishness of the Gospel* (Jerusalem: Jewish New Testament Publications, 1988); John Fischer, *If It Be of God* (Chicago: Messianic Jewish Alliance of America, 1975); idem, "Why a Messianic Movement?" *Trinity Journal*, Spring 1976; idem, "Messianic Jews Are Still Jews," *Christianity Today* (24 April 1981); idem, *The Olive Tree Connection* (Downers Grove, Ill.: InterVarsity Press, 1983).

[13]See, for example, Daniel Fuller, *Gospel and Law: Contrast or Continuum?* (Grand Rapids: Eerdmans, 1980).

by Paul, the rabbi and apostle. In Acts 23:6 and 26:5 Paul speaks as a Pharisee, and in 2 Corinthians 11:22 he addresses his readers from a stance within the Jewish community. These are positions of connection rather than "separation." Nor is the issue of "newness" quite so clear-cut. The terminology and context of Jeremiah 31–33; Hebrews 8; and Matthew 9:16–17 (the new covenant and new wine texts) certainly imply "renewed" things rather than things that are merely "new" and nothing more.[14] Further, in Romans 3:1–2; 9:3–5; and 11:29, Paul stresses the *present* reality—as well as the irrevocability—of the privilege and calling of the Jewish people and nation.

The phrase "outside the camp" (page 34) is misconstrued and therefore misused. "Outside the camp" in Exodus 33:7 describes the very heart of Judaism, the original Tent of Meeting. When God revealed himself to his people at Mount Sinai, he met them "out of the camp" (Exodus 19:17). "Outside the camp" is the place of ceremonial cleansing with the ashes of the red heifer (Numbers 19:9) and the location of significant elements of the Yom Kippur (Day of Atonement) ritual, as the bodies of the sacrifices are taken here and the scapegoat is released here (Leviticus 16:21–22, 27). So "outside the camp" serves as the core of Judaism and does not imply a separation from it.[15]

Varner—and Baron—wield Galatians 3:28 and Ephesians 2:11–22 as clubs against Messianic Judaism while ignoring a couple of vital factors. First, Messianic synagogues are far better expressions of the unity of believers in the Messiah than most churches because the presence of Jews and non-Jews is far more evenly distributed in Messianic congregations. Second, in Galatians 4–5 Paul clearly does *not* have "in mind Jewish as well as Gentile believers" (page 34). According to Galatians 5:2, he expressly addresses his comments to the "uncircumcised." Two further comments—both of these by Gentile scholars—are apropos at this point.

[14]See Walter Kaiser, "The Old Promise and the New Covenant," *Journal of the Evangelical Theological Society*, 15 (1972); John Fischer, "Covenant, Fulfillment and Judaism in Hebrews," in John Fischer, ed., *The Enduring Paradox* (Baltimore, Md.: Lederer, 2000); David H. Stern, *Jewish New Testament Commentary*, comments on Matthew 9:16–17 (Clarksville, Md.: Jewish New Testament Publications, 1992).

[15]For a more complete treatment, see Fischer, "Hebrews," in *The Enduring Paradox*. This may well involve some element of disparagement for the believers because of their identification with Yeshua as the Messiah.

> Paul never seems to have compelled the Gentile churches to act like Jews . . . , but it remains equally true that he does not expect Jewish churches to act like Gentile believers. He never says that it is wrong for them to be circumcised, or to keep the law, or to observe the festivals. All he insists is that these things have nothing to do with the gift of salvation.[16]

> The Jewish festivals foreshadow the Messiah and are fulfilled in Him. However, a shadow cannot highlight anyone, even the Messiah, if it is totally removed from the picture. The Jewish festivals are not obsolete but are good contemporary teachers. . . . Jewish ceremony will be pleasing in God's sight if done in the name of the One in whom all Jewish ceremonies are fulfilled.[17]

BIBLICAL-THEOLOGICAL CONCERNS

Varner's concerns in this arena are equally misplaced. To start with, he attempts to drive a wedge between Paul's past life in Judaism and his present life, an endeavor that Paul's own statements belie. In the passages cited earlier (Acts 23:6 and 26:5 and 2 Corinthians 11:22) Paul explicitly maintains his ongoing connection to Judaism as part of his present experience. How else could he have defended himself in Acts 28:17, toward the latter part of his life, by saying he had still "done nothing against . . . the customs [traditions] of our ancestors"? In other words, he claims to have been consistently observant of Judaism throughout his entire life. To escape the import of passages such as these, Varner constructs a false dichotomy between "being a Jew" and participation in "Judaism," a disjunction that may be relevant, at some levels, for the modern Western world but that functionally would have made little or no sense in the ancient Near Eastern world.[18] In addition, Varner anachronistically

[16]R. Alan Cole, *Epistle of Paul to the Galatians* (Grand Rapids: Eerdmans, 1965), 12. Also see John Fischer, "Galatians from a Messianic Jewish Perspective," *Messianic Outreach* (Autumn 1988–Summer 1989).

[17]Goble, *Everything You Need to Grow a Messianic Synagogue*, 10.

[18]Thorleif Boman, *Hebrew Thought Compared with Greek* (New York: W. W. Norton, 1960); John Fischer, "Beware of Greeks Bearing Gifts," *The Hebrew Christian* (Winter 1984).

speaks of "Judaism" when he should be referring to the "Judaisms" of this period.[19]

Even in Philippians 3, where Paul apparently speaks disparagingly of his life in Judaism, he nevertheless describes his Jewish connections in the present tense as a current experience. Contrary to Varner's assessment of this passage, the context does not indicate that Paul considers these things as "impediments"; he is merely stressing the comparative values of the two experiences—participation in Judaism and a relationship with the Messiah. When compared to *any* (and every) experience (verse 8), a relationship with Yeshua makes the others seem like "rubbish" in comparison, as the NIV nicely phrases this verse, picking up its intended nuances. This "exaggerated comparison" technique—a common rabbinic device—parallels Yeshua's own use of the technique in Luke 14:26. There Yeshua says that in comparison to a person's love for him, all other family affections and connections should appear as "hate." As Varner succinctly expresses it (page 37), Philippians 3 emphasizes Paul's conviction that "knowing Jesus as his Messiah was far more valuable than any of these privileges and accomplishments." This is exactly what Paul stresses, while at the same time he does not disavow his life in Judaism. To revise Varner's assessment, the rabbi-apostle clearly found his identity in the Jewish Messiah and also in his—and the Messiah's—Jewishness. Philippians 3:3 says as much: Paul is among those who *are* (still) the circumcision, who worship by the Spirit of God, and who glory in the Messiah Yeshua.

Varner engages in further hermeneutical gymnastics in his treatment of Acts 18:18 and 21:23–26. He is correct in saying (page 37) that these incidents "cannot be interpreted to contradict [Paul's] clear teaching [in his letters]." But, on closer examination, what these passages contradict is not Paul's teaching but Varner's own interpretation of Paul. In these passages—and others (e.g., Acts 20:6, 16; 27:9)—Paul enthusiastically participates

---

[19]See Gabriele Boccaccini, *Middle Judaism: Jewish Thought 300 B.C.E. to 200 C.E.* (Minneapolis: Fortress, 1991); Shaye Cohen, *From the Maccabees to the Mishnah* (Philadelphia: Westminster, 1987); E. P. Sanders, *Judaism: Practice and Belief 63 B.C.E.–66 C.E.* (London: SCM Press, 1992); Lawrence Schiffman, *From Text to Tradition: A History of Second Temple and Rabbinic Judaism* (Hoboken, N.J.: KTAV Publishing, 1991).

in Jewish rituals and ceremonies. The implications are so straightforward that Varner is compelled to explain them away by describing Paul's actions (page 37) as "illustrating *personal* choices rather than exemplifying a pattern of congregational worship. His actions have been 'overinterpreted' to justify a pattern of observance they were never intended to exemplify." Clearly it is Varner who is involved in "overinterpreting" Paul, who certainly understands the implications of his own letters as well as his own actions in Acts. After all, this is the same rabbi who repeatedly urged his disciples to imitate his example: "Whatever you have learned or received or heard from me, or seen in me—put it into practice" (Philippians 4:9; cf. 1 Corinthians 4:16; 11:1; Philippians 3:17; 2 Thessalonians 3:7, 9). This serves to answer Varner's question (page 38), "Where in the New Testament record can it be shown that the ritual practices of Second Temple Judaism ever characterized the congregational pattern of the early churches?" The answer is further confirmed by the patristic evidence of Epiphanius and Irenaeus (page 53) that both the apostles and their Nazarene followers "continued in the ancient observances" of Judaism. Clearly Paul—and the others—participated continuously and actively in Judaism, as numerous scholars have also observed.[20]

Varner appears to be unaware of *actual* Messianic congregations when he argues (page 38) that "Messianic Judaism tends to promote divisions . . ." As observed earlier in my response, in reality Messianic synagogues normally do a better job of picturing the unity of Yeshua's followers than most other congregations. Usually, it is only in Messianic congregations that a roughly equal proportion of Jews and Gentiles can be found. As for the red herring of "divisions," what *apparently* exhibits divisions in the Messiah's body more pointedly than the multitude of denominations that make up Varner's own Protestantism?

[20]For example, Philip Cunningham, *Jewish Apostle to the Gentiles: Paul As He Saw Himself* (Mystic, Conn.: Twenty-Third Publications, 1986); W. D. Davies, *Paul and Rabbinic Judaism* (London: SPCK, 1955); Timothy Hegg, *The Letter Writer* (Littleton, Colo.: First Fruits of Zion, 2002); Pinchas Lapide and Peter Stuhlmacher, *Paul, Rabbi and Apostle* (Minneapolis: Augsburg, 1984); E. P. Sanders, *Paul and Palestinian Judaism* (Philadelphia: Fortress, 1977); Peter Tomson, *Paul and the Jewish Law* (Minneapolis: Fortress, 1990).

Varner then goes on to misconstrue Ephesians 2:11–22 and misapply Galatians 3:28. As he correctly observes, the layout of the second temple serves as the metaphor or background for Ephesians 2:11–22. So the "barrier" (verse 14) refers to the fence of the Court of the Gentiles that kept them at some distance ("far away," verse 13) from the main temple structures. Yeshua tore down "the enmity" that this barrier illustrated; that fence was itself governed by "the Law of commandments contained in ordinances" (verse 15 NASB). With the metaphorical fence gone, Gentiles can come "near" (whereas they were formerly "far away") and together with the Jews "have access" (verse 18) to God, as pictured by temple participation.

Several observations are called for at this point. First, as the structure and context of this passage—as well as the Greek text itself—indicate, it was the "enmity," *not* "the Law" (verse 15 NASB), that Yeshua tore down. Second, the temple metaphor pictures Gentiles *coming into* the temple together with the Jews and does *not* imply that either group is *walking away from* the temple (or the practices it represents). If anything, the imagery illustrates movement toward, not away from, Jewish observances. This correlates precisely with the prophetic anticipation of Gentile involvement in the worship of "the God of Jacob" (Isaiah 2:2–3; Zechariah 8:20–23; 14:16–19). Third, the reader must be careful not to confuse the reality with the analogy. The temple serves as a metaphor or picture of the unity of Messianic believers; it is not itself the focus of Paul's discussion. So he is not describing what happens to the temple and its related observances; he is discussing the mutual relationship of Jews and Gentiles to God because of the Messiah. Therefore, according to Paul, the temple is not abolished; rather, God is accessed. Otherwise, without the existence of the tangible temple, the prophetic passages cited above cannot be accurately fulfilled. Fourth, it is not David H. Stern in his commentary who is involved in "bifurcation" and "special pleading" and "avoiding the plain reading of the text" (page 39); it is Varner. As it turns out, there is a distinct historical Jewish background and context to Stern's discussion of the ordinances, or takkanot. As George Foote Moore pointed out decades ago,

> Thus the distinctive religious institutions of Judaism as it was in the first centuries of our era were carried back to its

> beginnings. Ezra and the Men of the Great Synagogue were believed to have introduced these institutions and regulations by ordinances (takkanot) having the force of law.[21]

Further, the accuracy and antiquity of these traditions have been validated, as William F. Albright and Herschel Shanks, among others,[22] have pointed out. Albright makes this observation:

> We now know . . . that oral tradition in pre-Talmudic Jewish sources is often extraordinarily accurate even as far back as the Exilic period or earlier. The data contained in our rabbinic sources of the second century A.D. and later are proving reliable for earlier times than generally believed. The sayings of the leading Jewish teachers of the intertestamental and NT periods were preserved with remarkable tenacity for centuries after their original date.[23]

Herschel Shanks, editor of *Biblical Archaeology Review,* wrote this:

> The Dead Sea Scrolls are showing that the rabbinic texts are far more reliable than was previously thought. . . . From the Dead Sea Scrolls, we learn that methods of Pharisaic biblical interpretation and the development of the Oral (Talmudic) Law had begun long before Judaism was bereft of its Temple.[24]

So Varner's critique and his declaration that "these rabbinic decrees refer almost exclusively to much later decisions" (page 39) are "anachronistic," and *not* Stern's commentary. To rephrase Varner's own reflection (page 40), this illustrates the lengths to which some opponents of Messianic Judaism will go to explain

---

[21]George Foote Moore, *Judaism in the First Centuries of the Christian Era,* vol. 1 (New York: Schocken, 1971), 33.

[22]For example, David Flusser, *Judaism and the Origins of Christianity* (Jerusalem: Magnes Press, 1988); Shmuel Safrai, "Talmudic Literature as an Historical Source for the Second Temple Period," *Mishkan* (2/1992–3/1993).

[23]W. F. Albright and C. S. Mann, *Matthew: A New Translation with Introduction and Commentary,* Anchor Bible (New York: Doubleday, 1971), clxvi.

[24]Herschel Shanks, "Light on the 'New' Scrolls," Outlook, *The Washington Post* (19 April 1992).

away texts that clearly teach that observance of Jewish customs is appropriate for Messianic Jews.

Varner's handling of Galatians 3:28 is equally shortsighted. In his treatment he asks a leading question (page 40): "Shouldn't we urge our congregants to seek their identity in their Lord and not in their culture?" This makes an unsubstantiated assumption and builds on an unwarranted presupposition. Varner assumes that each specific local expression of the body of the Messiah must identically demonstrate the unity that is to be exhibited throughout the entire universal body. This is neither necessarily accurate nor even practically possible in all parts of the globe. Further, Varner supposes that there is some culturally neutral way to express worship. The proliferation of various Asian and Hispanic congregations, let alone African-American ones, in the United States alone indicates the fallacy of presuming that forms of worship and religious expression are culturally neutral. Numerous Christian scholars have addressed this very issue.[25]

Next, the argument that "Messianic Judaism emphasizes the 'shadow' of Old Testament typical, or symbolic, practices" rather than "the 'reality' of New Testament fulfillments" (page 41) constructs a false and misleading dichotomy. It assumes that the two cannot be appropriately integrated, which clearly *can be* and has been done in Messianic synagogues. Further, the use of Colossians 2:16–17 in this part of the discussion is most inappropriate, as this passage is clearly not addressed to Jews. Verse 18 describes the "worship of angels" as part of the practice of his readers. There is no record of any Jewish sect ever worshiping angels, or, for that matter, involving themselves in "self-abasement" (verse 18 NASB) either. Clearly, the Colossian problem was *not* a Jewish problem but more likely a Gnostic-related problem.

Varner then asks (page 41), "Now that we have the 'substance' ..., why would anyone encourage others to continue to

---

[25]For example, David Hesselgrave, *Communicating Christ Cross-Culturally* (Grand Rapids: Zondervan, 1991); idem, *Planting Churches Cross-Culturally* (Grand Rapids: Baker, 2000); Marvin Mayers, *Christianity Confronts Culture* (Grand Rapids: Zondervan, 1987); Eugene Nida, *Customs and Cultures* (New York: Harper & Row, 1959).

practice the shadow?" Part of the answer is found in his subsequent quotation from F. F. Bruce: "If a Christian wishes to restrict himself in matters of food and drink, or to set apart days for special observance or commemoration, good and well." Another reason, as pointed out earlier in my response (page 55), is that a shadow or pointer cannot reflect or highlight anyone if it is removed from the picture. So it remains a good contemporary teacher, as even Varner concedes (page 43): "To use these 'shadows' as wonderful teaching tools is well and good." After all, the shadow and reality are irrevocably and organically connected; the shadow is part of the ongoing reality and cannot be divorced from its "substance."

Varner's discussion of Hebrews is similarly suspect. For example, Westcott makes this observation in his commentary:

> Prominence is assigned in the epistle to the Old Testament, both to the writing and to the institutions it hallows. There is not the least tendency towards disparagement of the one or the other. . . .
>
> From first to last it is maintained that God spoke to the fathers in the prophets. The message through the son takes up and crowns all that had gone before.[26]

Further, Hebrews 8:13, despite its usual interpretations, does speak of Jewish observance in the present tense. Hebrews 9:9 describes Jewish practices as pictures for "the present time." And Hebrews 10:1 literally mentions "the good things that are coming."[27] Therefore, to argue that these practices "have been replaced" (page 43) misses the point of Hebrews entirely.

As for the temporality of the shadow, for which Varner argues, Exodus 12:14, 17, 24; 31:13, 16–17, among numerous other passages, certainly seem to indicate otherwise. These passages repeatedly speak of the "forever" and "lasting" nature of these practices. Varner also misunderstands Messianic synagogues when he weighs in on the "impression" left that Messianic Judaism views these practices "as matters of religious obligation."

---

[26]B. F. Westcott, *The Epistle to the Hebrews* (Grand Rapids: Eerdmans, 1970), lviii, lxi.

[27]For a more complete discussion, see Fischer, "Hebrews," in *The Enduring Paradox*.

Neither Messianic Judaism[28] nor for that matter Classical Judaism properly understood[29] operates from a legalistic perspective. Rather, there is an emphasis on God's graciousness and people's response in gratitude, on religious observance being a matter of sensational opportunity rather than slavish obligation. Psalms 19 and 119 beautifully illustrate and elaborate this perspective. Varner (page 43) then exhorts Messianic Jews that, because of their identification with Yeshua, "they must be willing to suffer." Unfortunately they often do—as a result of the misunderstandings of well-meaning Christians.

Varner next expresses a concern about which he is uncertain: that Messianic Jews in their effort to accurately reflect the biblical teaching of the triune nature of God in a Jewish way will stray into "limiting the full deity of Messiah" (page 43). A couple of observations are necessary at this point. While the "doctrines so carefully hammered out at Nicea and Chalcedon" are clearly biblical, their descriptions by those councils are not similarly divinely inspired. Mainstream Messianic Judaism has repeatedly reaffirmed both the triune nature of God and the deity of Yeshua.[30] Interestingly, there have been some within Christianity who have stepped back from these same affirmations.[31] Therefore, this concern is much more of a red herring than a reality.

HISTORICAL AND PRAGMATIC CONCERNS

Due to space considerations the discussion of this section will be quite brief. Varner begins by stating the obvious, that "it

---

[28]See, for example, the "Statement of Faith" of the Union of Messianic Jewish Congregations.

[29]See Roger Brooks, *The Spirit of the Ten Commandments: Shattering the Myth of Rabbinic Legalism* (San Francisco: Harper & Row, 1990); Solomon Schechter, *Aspects of Rabbinic Theology* (New York: Schocken, 1972); Roy Stewart, *Rabbinic Theology* (Edinburgh: Oliver and Boyd, 1961); John Fischer, "The Place of Rabbinic Tradition in a Messianic Jewish Lifestyle," in Fischer, ed., *The Enduring Paradox*.

[30]For example, see the "Statement of Faith" of the Union of Messianic Jewish Congregations.

[31]A prime example is Anthony Buzzard and Charles Hunting, *The Doctrine of the Trinity: Christianity's Self-Inflicted Wound* (Morrow, Ga.: Atlanta Bible College, 1994).

is simply impossible to return to the same situation that Jewish believers faced in apostolic times" (page 44). However, the ramifications he derives from this observation are troublesome. By claiming that "we simply cannot utilize arguments from Acts that are tied to that system" (page 44), he effectively nullifies the direct relevance of Acts, and by implication the gospels, to the twenty-first century. He makes Acts simply a transitional book that is not intended to address and apply to modern times and that functions only as a historical record. However, a large number of Paul's epistles were written during this same "transitional period"; are they likewise to be relegated to the dustbin of history? This approach smacks of a rather subjective use and prioritizing of Scripture.

Then Varner cites the introduction of the *Birkat HaMinim* into the *shemoneh esreh* as evidence of the final—and from his perspective, appropriate—"parting of the ways" between the Classical and Messianic Jewish communities, the "final rejection" of the Messianic Jews by the larger Jewish community (page 45). But this "evidence" is by no means clear-cut, as Anthony Saldarini notes:

> For example, the *Birkat Ha-Minim* . . . cannot be reliably dated to the late first or second centuries, nor shown to have been generally used in the Jewish communities, nor proved to have been aimed at Christians. Thus it cannot be identified as a cause for the expulsion of followers of Jesus from the synagogue.[32]

The description of the Talmud should be determinative at this point. It refers to this "blessing" as *Birkat HaTsedukim* (referring to the Sadducees) throughout (Berachot 28d–29a). The statements of Epiphanius and Irenaeus cited earlier in my response

[32]Anthony Saldarini, "Bible Books," *Bible Review* (April 1996): 40. See also Reuven Kimelman, "*Birkat Ha-Minim* and the Lack of Evidence for an Anti-Christian Prayer in Late Antiquity," in E. P. Sanders, ed., *Jewish and Christian Self-Definition*, vol. 2 (Philadelphia: Fortress, 1981), 226–44; Geza Vermes, *Post-Biblical Jewish Studies* (Leiden: E. J. Brill, 1975); Israel Abrahams, "By the (Expressed) Name," in Gedaliah Alon, ed., *Jews, Judaism, and the Classical World* (Jerusalem: Magnes Press, 1977); Flusser, *Judaism and the Origins of Christianity;* John Fischer, "Yeshua and Halakhah: Which Direction?" a paper available from Menorah Ministries, Palm Harbor, Florida.

(pages 52–53) confirm the continuity of the two communities beyond the second century.

In addition, Varner maintains that "the idea that Messianic synagogues are a more effective witness to the Jewish community ignores historical realities. There are no hard statistics to prove this idea" (page 46). He then declares, "Another historical reality is that most members of Messianic synagogues were led to the Lord by Gentile believers." While this statement may be comforting and comfortable to Varner, it is by no means convincing. It lacks the same "hard statistics" he finds lacking for the effectiveness of Messianic synagogues. He then laments the change of position on Messianic Judaism by some leaders of traditional Jewish missions and asks (page 46): "What happened to cause these and other leaders to change their positions?" The answer may well be: more careful study of Scripture and clearer thinking!

Finally, Varner authoritatively declares, "By emphasizing so many nonbiblical Jewish observances, Messianic Judaism falls under Jesus' condemnation of the oral law of the Pharisees" (page 47). This unfortunately ignores the many nonbiblical but nevertheless appropriate traditions—which he hints at—found in many churches and denominations. It also distorts Yeshua's message quite clearly spelled out in Matthew 23. Here Yeshua condemns *not* the oral law, *not* the Pharisees, *but only* the hypocrites among some Pharisees (whom they themselves, in fact, also harshly condemn in the pages of the Talmud [Sotah 20a–22b; Yevamot 16a]). Furthermore, in the beginning of Matthew 23 (verses 2–3), Yeshua pointedly instructs his followers to practice all that the Pharisees teach!

In his "A Concluding Model," Varner approvingly cites Arnold Fruchtenbaum as support for his ideal of a "Hebrew Christian fellowship within a church" (page 48). Interestingly, Fruchtenbaum's contribution to this volume argues for the Messianic congregation! Varner's concluding comments are quite problematic: "We need congregations like Antioch that do not just say 'Gentiles are welcome' but proclaim a Messiah who is for all men and women ... where the center of their fellowship is not culture but Christ" (page 49). Those who have spent significant time in Messianic synagogues have observed the genuine welcome and reception accorded to Gentiles there and have noted the clarity and the centrality of Yeshua and his message. No specific denominational or evangelical church or theology has a monopoly on the effective presentation of God's gospel.

Yes, we certainly *do* need Messianic synagogues. God used them powerfully in the past, he is using them effectively in the present, and he apparently intends to do so in the future as well.

A DANGER OF THROWING OUT THE BABY WITH THE BATH WATER

A Response to William Varner

Arnold G. Fruchtenbaum

There is much in William Varner's chapter that I can and do agree with and that mirrors my own critique on the movement in my chapter in this book as well as in my writings elsewhere. Therefore, I am not unsympathetic about his concerns. He has clearly spelled out, correctly, key problems within the movement, and his criticisms are valid for certain types of Messianic congregations. However, I do not think he has proven his case that therefore all forms of Messianic congregations are wrong and should be abandoned. In other words, he has made a valid case against certain types of Messianic congregations (the same would be true for certain types of Gentile churches), but has he made a case against biblically based Messianic congregations where these criticisms would not apply? My response to this question is that he has not. If there is one common problem I see in Varner's chapter, it is the tendency to throw out the baby with the bath water.

POINTS OF AGREEMENT

Let me begin with points of agreement, though some come with certain reservations.

1. Varner is correct in that there is no going back and recreating the Messianic context of the first century, especially its pre-A.D. 70 period. To claim a return to "the New Testament church" or to "first-century Messianic Judaism" is nothing but wishful thinking. The fact is, we do not have sufficient detailed information or documents to know exactly how a first-century Messianic congregation functioned or how diverse congregations, Jewish or Gentile, were within that first-century period. For example, the style of worship may include dancing today, but referring to it as "Davidic dance" is wishful thinking since much of what is passed off as Davidic dance has its roots in Eastern European culture rather than first-century Middle Eastern culture. There is no evidence that dancing was part of the worship service (any more than it is part of the average Orthodox Jewish service on the Sabbath today), and furthermore it would never happen in that context that men and women would dance together. I agree that all ancient claimed origins of some modern-day Messianic Jewish practices are wishful thinking. This does not make the actions themselves wrong, but only that the claimed antiquity is questionable.

2. It is also true that the only usage of the term "Judaism" in Paul's writings mentions it as being something in Paul's past and not in Paul's present. It is also true that "this does not mean that Paul thought he had ceased to be a Jew" (page 36). This does seem to show that Paul distinguished between "Judaism" and "Jewishness" and that the leaving of one does not mean the leaving of the other. It is also true that, as Paul compares what he has in the Messiah to what he had in Judaism, the comparison is that what he had in Judaism he declared "rubbish," since none of the elements of Judaism did anything for his eternal salvation. But what he says is "rubbish" is only in comparison to what is so much greater—not that the thing itself is by nature "rubbish." Based on the criterion of what constitutes the means of salvation, everything else is "rubbish"; and I would include in this category things like baptism and the Lord's Table. However, if viewed from a totally different criterion, is either practice "rubbish"? Obviously not.

3. I would especially agree that "those practices that some Messianic Jews emphasize so strongly are the very things that can often lead to self-righteousness and actual loss of the real knowledge of the Messiah" (page 37). I have frequently observed

this myself. However, it does not always follow. There are also valid biblical practices of the New Testament church that can lead some to self-righteousness as well, and yet this does not make this practice itself illegitimate. Having attended two Christian schools where there was a great deal of legalism, I noticed that abstention from wine, dancing, going to movies, and playing with dice in a Monopoly game also led to self-righteousness and the obscuring of what it means to be free in the Messiah. Yet it is possible both to participate and to abstain without developing self-righteousness.

4. I strongly agree with Varner's critique about how some Messianic Jewish leaders, including David H. Stern (see pages 39–41), raise some real problems when trying to avoid the clear teaching that the Mosaic law is no longer the mandatory rule of life for believers. A careful exegesis of Ephesians 2:11–22 is necessary. I would have to say that an honest Messianic Jewish commentary on the New Testament has yet to be written.

5. As my own chapter will show, I fully agree that the law of Moses came to an end at Messiah's death as a mandatory rule of life. This includes the two elements that Varner mentioned: the dietary restrictions and the festival observances (page 41). But is it wrong to continue dietary restrictions and the festivals, even if they cannot be followed in the exact format required by the Mosaic law? Does a Jewish believer *have* to eat the ham sandwich? Is it a *sin* for a Jewish believer to observe the Passover? Here again it seems to me we have "the baby with the bath water" motif repeating itself.

6. I fully agree that "Messianic Jews will never be able to please Jewish religious leaders today, no matter how 'Jewish' they try to be" (page 43). Jewish believers are deceiving themselves if they think that taking on a more Jewish lifestyle will make them more acceptable to the Jewish community. The final issue will not be "Torah observance" but the issue of the messiahship of Jesus. It is self-deceiving to believe that a Jewish lifestyle is the means of being accepted by the Jewish community or the Jewish leaders. However, from my perspective, this was never a valid reason to establish Messianic congregations to begin with.

7. Also agreed on is the fallacy that "Messianic synagogues are a more effective witness to the Jewish community" (page 46). This has not been true historically. Now that the Messianic

congregations have been around for about thirty years, it is still not proven that this is the most effective way of winning Jewish people to the Messiah. It is very obvious that the majority of Jewish members of Messianic congregations came to the Lord in other ways—by means of Gentiles witnessing to them and, in most cases, not in a particularly "Jewish way." However, it is also my perspective that this was never the primary purpose for having a Messianic congregation anyway.

8. I thoroughly agree that there is a distinct danger when we make nonbiblical Jewish traditions "part of the worship ordinances and give the impression that they are what God desires us to do. Immature believers do not always have the discernment to distinguish between preference and commands" (page 47). This, too, is one of my own criticisms in that many Messianic believers fail to distinguish what is purely tradition from what is a biblical imperative and consequently go on to turn traditions into imperatives.

But this is not a problem unique to Messianic congregations, since all churches have traditions that at times appear to be mandatory. I would like to see Varner expand on the traditions of Gentile churches and how he would handle them. I would love to see him write an article that discusses the church's traditions around Christmas and Easter. Would he defend some of these practices or not? If he would, what would be the basis for doing so? If he would negate them, would he call for removal of these practices from the church?

Here again, the fact that some people draw faulty conclusions based on certain practices does not make the practices themselves wrong. They must be judged on their own merit and not on how people misconstrue them. For example, some churches teach that baptism is mandatory for salvation, but this would not negate baptism as a practice simply because some misconstrue it. Baptism is not a tradition but a command of the Lord. But what about the many traditions that churches have, especially when some have been misinterpreted by a legalism that can take different forms? Would Varner negate the practice of legitimate traditions simply because of conclusions reached about them by some people?

9. Finally, Varner expresses a concern I also share, namely, that elements in the Messianic movement are moving toward a

heretical theology that would include a denial of the Trinity and a denial of the deity of the Messiah (pages 43–44). This tie to Ebionism is quite real and, from my observation, even growing. Such dangers, however, do not negate the concept of Messianic congregations, and the proper counteraction is solid Bible teaching, no different from what it would be in other churches. The lack of solid Bible teaching in the movement is appalling. Many of the leaders in the Messianic movement became leaders by virtue of their personalities rather than their solid biblical and theological training and education. Often the poor theology among many of the mainline members is due mostly to a lack of exposure to good teaching.

The Jewish ministry Varner once served with chose to totally separate themselves.[1] They had no presence at Messianic conventions and conferences and thus were not there to give their input. As a result many new Jewish believers made the assumption that there is only one option—the option they were being exposed to. They were not hearing about anything else. It should be noted that just as faith comes by hearing, by the same token solid Bible teaching also comes by hearing. If that ministry and others like it had not chosen a total separation, thus depriving the movement of good, solid Bible doctrine, the problem would not have been as acute as it has come to be at the present time. I pray that the newly formed Association of Messianic Congregations will make a major contribution toward overcoming what is lacking in sound theology in the movement—an issue that greatly troubles both Dr. Varner and me.

POINTS OF DISAGREEMENT

Having noted the above points of agreement, either totally or partially, showing I am not totally unsympathetic with Varner's concerns, I now must note points of disagreement where I believe his criticisms are not valid—or not valid in their entirety—since they are generalized too much (as Varner himself admits to painting "with a broad brush"). The issue is not that what he says is untrue with reference to a good number of

[1]Friends of Israel Gospel Ministry.

Messianic congregations. However, it is not true of many others, so here again I point out the danger of throwing out the baby with the bath water.

1. Varner's strategy appears at times to consist of asking a question, with the implication that there is something fundamentally wrong with practicing the content of the question. One such question is, "How, then, can modern Messianic Jews desire to take part in the rituals of their pre-Messiah life?" (page 36). My counterquestion would be, "Is there something wrong with such a desire?" It certainly would be wrong if a Messianic Jew believed this was part of the salvation package, or a means of sanctification, or a means of pleasing God, or a practice that is mandatory. However, if a Messianic Jew realizes that he is not obligated to do these and that he is free from these things, can he not still use his freedom to practice them? In other words, what is biblically wrong with continuing such practices if they are New Testament-neutral and do not violate any New Testament imperatives?

If it is wrong to continue practicing certain rituals, this must be proven exegetically from the text and not by merely asking questions that carry presuppositions. I do not believe that Varner has proven his case exegetically. The quotation of Philippians 3:4–8 does not forbid the practice of these rituals, for Paul is only arguing against their value in either salvation or sanctification.

Here I go back to my earlier observation of distinguishing between Judaism and Jewishness. Judaism is a religious system, a system that views certain things as mandatory and has for its key base the rejection of the messiahship of Jesus. However, that is not the case with the practice of Jewishness. Different ethnic groups and cultures have different modes of expression, and there is no reason to assume that, while other ethnic groups and cultures may have their way of expressing their Christianity, Messianic Jews may not. It's possible for every ethnic group to have practices that are antibiblical, and a believer from that ethnic/cultural background would be required to abandon such practices. But if these practices are New Testament-neutral, then is he not free to practice them? Why should Jewish believers be held to a standard not imposed on others?

The book of Acts indicates more than once that Paul had no problem falling back on specific rituals and practices that did not contradict his own epistles. Varner admits that Paul indeed "observed certain Jewish rituals such as the Nazirite vow," then goes on to say, "These incidents, however, cannot be interpreted to contradict his clear teaching in Galatians and Philippians" (page 37). This is true. And it is exactly my point. What Paul did choose to do did not violate anything he said in his epistles. There are many things in the Mosaic law and/or Jewish tradition that do not violate any specific teachings of the New Testament. If Paul felt free to practice some of these, why would it be wrong for Jewish believers today to do the same? Varner is correct in that Paul did not view these things as being mandatory but matters of "personal choices," and this is also exactly my point. Not all Messianic congregations see these things as being mandatory but rather as purely optional. If they are optional, then why would they be biblically wrong?

Varner believes that Paul's actions "have been 'overinterpreted' to justify a pattern of observance they were never intended to exemplify" (page 37). This is a true statement as well. The New Testament does not command us to follow Paul's examples on the choices he made. On the other hand, it does not forbid other believers to make similar choices as long as they do not make them mandatory for others. After all, there is an equal danger of "underinterpretation" that would then prohibit Jewish believers from making similar choices with their freedom in the Messiah. Is it possible for a Messianic congregation to have a form of Jewish expression that does not contradict anything Paul says in Galatians and Philippians? The answer is yes, and there are such congregations in existence—including the one I attend.

Varner's brush is indeed too broad and implies that all Messianic congregations fall into the same error with only perhaps a few exceptions, but exceptions are much more numerous than he might think. I regret that the "exceptions" have not had an equal voice in the two major Messianic conventions that take place annually, but the views expressed in these conventions are not unanimous—though perhaps they may be held by the majority. But just as there are Baptist churches I would recommend and Baptist churches I would not recommend, the same is true with Messianic congregations.

2. Varner devotes considerable space to the issue of the dividing wall of hostility, with the implication that having separate

Messianic congregations creates the "appearance that the wall still separates us" (page 39). The original wall of separation made a clear distinction between Jews and Gentiles in the context of the second temple worship system. As Varner states, such a wall can never come back up because it has been broken down forever, but he seems to feel that the practice of Messianic Jewishness and Messianic congregations would give the "appearance" the wall is still erect by separating Jewish and Gentile believers.

This criticism would be absolutely valid if we were dealing with a situation where Messianic congregations were "for Jews only" and there was a bylaw that said "Gentile Christians need not apply," but I do not know of a single Messianic congregation where this would be a ruling. As far as I know, every Messianic congregation has Gentile members, and in a great number of them (if not the majority of them) there are more Gentile members than Jewish ones. I even know of some that are totally Gentile without a single Jewish member. Even the "rabbi" is a Gentile. That being the case, Messianic congregations are hardly guilty of re-creating the dividing wall separating Jews from Gentiles.

The situation here, then, has to do with a chosen style of worship and practice rather than with creating a wall of division. On this issue, what would be the difference between a Baptist church that has both Jewish and Gentile believers in it and a Messianic congregation that has both Jewish and Gentile believers in it? Both Jews and Gentiles share the membership equally and the leadership equally. The key difference has more to do with the style of worship and the Jewish emphasis, with one having a more Jewish expression than the other.

The fact is that today the church is fragmented along ethnic lines, theological lines, and many more lines. Thus, different churches have different forms of expression. The variety of expressions in themselves are not wrong; and each local congregation, whatever country they may be in or whatever ethnic group they may come from, will be influenced by their cultural background with respect to the type of services they have. The same thing is true of Jewish congregations. There is no basis for pronouncing that Jewish believers are the only ones who are not allowed to have their own ethnic congregations. There are blacks in predominantly white churches, but there are blacks who prefer to be in predominantly black churches with their own ethnic expression entering into the style of worship. A white Baptist church and a black Baptist church may both be Baptist and located in the same country—even the same state—yet their form of worship can differ widely. By the same token there are Jews in predominantly Gentile churches and there are Jews who prefer to have their own ethnic expression in their worship services. Unless there is something fundamentally exegetically wrong, there is no biblical basis to forbid it.

In citing Galatians 3:28, Varner does not do what so many have done in interpreting the passage to mean that all distinctions between Jews and Gentiles have been erased. In applying it to Messianic congregations, he points out that, just as this verse does not justify having a church for men, a church for women, a church for masters, and a church for slaves, it does not justify having a church for Jews and a church for Gentiles. Again he raises an objection in the form of a question, "If it is necessary to establish Jewish congregations to accommodate Jewish believers, is it necessary to establish slave congregations or female congregations to also meet their needs?" (page 40).

This is a valid observation insofar as it goes. This verse cannot be used to justify separate congregations, nor does it teach that it is *necessary* to have Jewish congregations. But the real question is this: Are such congregations forbidden? The fact that there are no separate churches for women or for slaves is not by itself a prohibition against Messianic congregations. Furthermore, most churches, especially larger ones, do have separate fellowships for men, women, children, and teenagers, recognizing a need for these divisions. The fact is that, for the most part, churches—even those with Jewish members—have not seen a need to have Messianic fellowships. Again, no valid exegesis of Galatians 3:28 would prohibit having Messianic congregations.

Varner goes on to ask another question, "Shouldn't we urge our congregants to seek their identity in their Lord and not in their culture?" (page 40). The answer, obviously, is yes. The fact is, no one can escape his or her culture. Whatever church Dr. Varner goes to, the style of worship in that church is based on a specific cultural context. Being a multicultural country, the United States has a variety of culture-oriented churches. Why would it be prohibited for Messianic Jews to have something similar?

It is a false dichotomy to pit seeking identity in the Lord against a specific cultural style of worship and practice. By all means, all Messianic Jews and all Gentiles of any color should seek their identity in the Lord. But what kind of worship style and congregation they choose is based on a specific culture—and there is no way to avoid this. If blacks are comfortable in a white-culture church, that is where they should stay. If they feel more comfortable in a black-culture church, they should have the option of attending such a congregation, as long as that church would not prohibit white members. The same thing is true with Messianic Jews. If they are content in a Gentile-culture church, that is where they should stay. If they wish to be part of a Messianic congregation to express their Jewish culture, that should be their option, as long as that congregation does not prohibit Gentile members.

Varner quotes F. F. Bruce, who points out that believers have been freed from the obligations of festival observances and food laws. But the same quotation goes on to say, "If a Christian wishes to restrict himself in matters of food and drink, or to set apart days for special observance or commemoration, good and well.... But to regard them as matters of religious obligation is a retrograde step for Christians to take" (page 41). Again, this is exactly the point. If a Messianic congregation makes these things mandatory, they are as wrong as churches that make Sunday observances mandatory. If it is a matter of free choice, then, as F. F. Bruce has stated, "good and well." There are Messianic congregations like ours that do make it a matter of personal choice, and therefore there is no valid argument against such a Messianic congregation.

3. Varner makes a rather bold statement that "Jewish believers today are not part of [the] Jewish community" (page 45). This statement is based on his previous comment that "the Jewish community does have the right to define who belongs to that community." I do not think this can be biblically defended. A study of the concept of "the remnant of Israel" from both Testaments clearly shows that the remnant is always part of the nation and not separated from the nation. Therefore, the remnant has always been part of the Jewish community. In Romans 11:5 Paul declares that even today there is a remnant of Israel. Therefore, Messianic Jews do have a dual citizenship: They are

members of the church and members of the Jewish community. It is irrelevant what the larger Jewish community feels about Messianic Jews. The remnant, theologically, is always part of the nation, not detached from the nation. The Bible, rather than what the rabbinic community thinks, is the authority for us concerning our identity.

4. Varner makes the observation that there were organizations in the past, such as Chosen People Ministries, that objected to Messianic congregations; he now asks the question, "What happened to cause these and other leaders to change their positions?" (page 46). The question is easy to answer. At the time of the opposition, which was basically in the mid-1970s, there was only one model of a Messianic congregation, exactly the model Varner objects to in his chapter. These were too rabbinically oriented, making the Mosaic law and many rabbinic traditions mandatory and claiming that they as a congregation were really part of Judaism and not a part of the church. Many theologically educated and biblically oriented Jewish believers could not accept that kind of a model. Since it was the only model, they rejected it out of hand, as was correct to do.

However, in the course of time other Messianic Jews, primarily workers with Chosen People Ministries and some with Ariel Ministries, offered a totally different model of a Messianic congregation that was biblically oriented. Now there was another model that took the Bible as its final authority and priority and built a Messianic congregation on the foundation of sound biblical theology. Now that there was a more biblically oriented model available, these ministries, while still not in favor of the first model, could very easily support the second model. They were therefore able to meet the desire of many Jewish believers who were not comfortable either with a Gentile-culture church or with a Messianic congregation of the first model. That was the reason, then, for the change in position.

5. As for the charge that taking Jewish believers away from good churches would add to the "Gentilization" (page 47) of the church, again that would be a valid critique if Messianic congregations were mandating Jewish members only. I for one am in favor of Jewish believers remaining in a good Bible-teaching church if there is no good Bible-teaching Messianic congregation available. Even if there is one available, this should only be a

matter of personal preference apart from any mandate for the Jewish believer to leave the church to join the Messianic congregation. The first priority must be the view of Scripture. As I have stated, I have often directed Jewish believers to churches to get solid Bible teaching in instances where I do not trust the theology of the local Messianic congregation. Where there are the options of Bible-centered Messianic congregations, I prefer to see a Jewish believer be part of one of those congregations than to be a member of a Gentile church where poor teaching goes on.

6. The accusation that "the more Messianic synagogues that develop, the more the church is relieved of its mission obligation to reach out to the Jewish people in evangelism and discipleship" (page 47) appears to me to be a make-believe problem. If a church uses such an excuse, it is only that—an excuse. I am reminded of the members of a church located near a university campus who felt they had no obligation to reach out to the student population because that ministry was being done by groups such as Navigators and Campus Crusade. That was just a make-believe excuse. The existence of campus ministries does not exempt a church from reaching out to university students if the students are part of their circle of influence. By the same token, the existence of Jewish missions ministries, of which Varner was once a part, did not negate the church's responsibility to reach out to Jewish communities themselves. The existence of Messianic congregations no more relieves the church of its responsibilities to do Jewish evangelism and discipleship than Jewish missions programs would. I think this objection is a bit of a stretch.

7. Finally, with respect to traditions, Varner warns against "the danger of adding to the Word of God, even unwittingly" (page 47). He admits, "All churches have traditions." But the real issue is this: Are these traditions made mandatory or not? If they are not mandatory, and if they do not violate New Testament revelation, then they become a valid option. If Gentile churches are allowed their Gentile traditions, Jewish believers should be allowed theirs. Jewish traditions should not be judged any differently from any other traditions. Two questions should be asked about any traditional practice within any kind of a congregation, Jewish or Gentile. The first: Does it violate any New Testament teaching? The second: Is it being made mandatory? If the answer

to both questions is no, then it becomes purely a matter of freedom of practice.

Varner ends his article with "a concluding model," and I have nothing personally against this model and have encouraged it myself in the past and continue to do so to the present. When I originally proposed that model (published in 1974), it was in response to the only other model of a Messianic congregation available at the time, as mentioned earlier in my response (page 76). Since then, other models have come forward. If Varner had quoted from my later work, he would have noted that, while I still support the model I presented in 1974, I also believe there is an equally valid second option, the option I present in my own chapter later in this volume.

LIVING THE MESSIANIC JEWISH LIFESTYLE

A Response to William Varner

Louis Goldberg

In discussion with some prominent Christian leaders concerning the specific needs of Messianic Jews, I was once told that the church had all the resources needed to care for all Jewish folks who accept the Messiah Jesus. I asked about the special cultural needs such as observing the Jewish holidays, using a liturgy that reflects both the Hebrew Scriptures and traditions compatible with the Word, perhaps even using a contextualized version of the Jewish liturgy, or *siddur.* I was asked, "Really? Is all this necessary?" The rejoinder continued, "They all speak English; the church has what is necessary from the Word of God to fulfill whatever need Jewish believers have. Why must we turn back from what Jesus has delivered us?"

I have had many an occasion to reflect on that response and tried to imagine (with hope) that not many Christians today would adopt such a sharp attitude against the many Jewish believers who do worship in congregations with a distinctively Messianic Jewish lifestyle. They seek to share what Yeshua the Messiah taught and what the Hebrew Scriptures (Old Testament) and New Covenant (New Testament) proclaim.

Fortunately, most missiologists today not only allow but insist that believers within each country or within each cultural expression have the right to contextualize their faith and lifestyle in accordance with their cultural background, as long as no basic biblical doctrine or teaching of Yeshua (Jesus) is ever twisted. David Hesselgrave notes, "Contextualization, then, is not simply nice. It is necessary. Without it, God's truth would never have broken out of the Hebrew community and into the larger world."[1] Here Hesselgrave refers to what *Sha'ul* (Paul) did when he took the message from the Jewish background to a non-Jewish one. Grant Osborne offers a general working definition of contextualization: "Contextualization comprises a dynamic process which attempts to interpret the significance of a religion or cultural norm for a group with a different, or 'developed,' cultural heritage."[2]

As I noted in the introduction to this book (page 13), the church today reflects in its theological pronouncements a Yeshua message contextualized in a Greek cultural form by the general church councils, from Nicea (A.D. 325) to Chalcedon (A.D. 451). At Nicea, worship was officially changed to occur on Sunday instead of the Sabbath, and Easter took the place of Passover. But in the original setting in the land of Israel there was a "Jewish" body of believers. As long as the message was being taught and lived by Yeshua in Israel, it was adapted and became entwined with many of the various models within the Jewish culture itself.[3] Those Messianic Jews who remained true to this message shared it over the next three to four hundred years (at least) with their brethren. But the message of the Messianic believers reflected that something new had occurred through the ministry of Yeshua, and then later, for sure, with the destruction of the temple in A.D. 70.

---

[1]David Hesselgrave, *Communicating Christ Cross-Culturally* (Grand Rapids: Zondervan, 1978), 84–85.

[2]Grant Osborne, *The Hermeneutical Spiral, A Comprehensive Introduction to Biblical Interpretation* (Downer's Grove, Ill.: InterVarsity Press, 1991), 318.

[3]For more on the beliefs and lifestyle of early Jewish believers, see Bellarmino Bagatti, *The Church from the Circumcision* (Jerusalem: Franciscan Printing Press, 1971).

UNIVERSALISM OR PARTICULARISM

Israel Prior to the Year 70

We need to consider how the leaders of the groups representing various religious beliefs viewed each other because of the differences of opinions within the nation, as well as how all these groups related to non-Jewish peoples. Two possibilities were present: universalism and particularism. Some of the Jewish religious bodies near the end of the second temple period in the days of Yeshua were: Pharisees; Sadducees; the people of Qumran (the Dead Sea Scroll community); Essenes; and the purveyors who penned the literature of the *sifrim hisonim* (Outside Books, or the Apocrypha and Pseudepigrapha)—these were groups representing a number of different views of a number of individuals. What's important to note is that a universalism existed. No one group pointed the finger at any other and said, "You are not Jewish anymore!" The situation changed somewhat during the Council of Yavneh (70–90), as already noted, when Jewish believers were put out of the synagogues because of their belief in Yeshua.

But today the situation is far different, especially among the orthodox Jewish community that says at times to liberals, conservatives, Reform Jews, Reconstructionists, and Messianic Jews alike, "You are no longer Jews!" The attitude is now very particularistic.

Universalism within the Body of Messiah

Let us go back to the setting of the Jerusalem council, which met to decide in about the year 50 the status of non-Jewish people who also desired to join with the Jewish believers. What was the general response of the religious leaders within the nation (as well as even a few in the body of Messiah)? Some of the believers at the council belonged to the party of the Pharisees, and they declared, "The Gentiles must be circumcised and required to obey the law of Moses" (Acts 15:5). They were only following the established particularistic custom for non-Jewish people who wanted to be part of the people of Israel. If these non-Jewish believers wanted to go further, they would have to adopt the Mosaic covenant and its traditional understanding and become full Jews.

The majority in the council at Jerusalem, certainly the leadership—*Ya'akov* (James), *Kefa* (Peter), as well as *Sha'ul* (Paul)—already realized that a new day was dawning. They adopted a universalistic position for the status of Jewish and non-Jewish believers within the body of the Messiah. For the former, as long as the second temple stood, they could go there and worship while also proclaiming Yeshua as the Messiah. Once the temple was destroyed, however, a crisis occurred in Israel's religious establishment as to what worship would now entail, and the Yavneh decision makers took up the challenge, as will be noted later in this chapter.

With this new universalism regarding the model of worship (the holidays) and lifestyle (the dietary laws and the multitude of practices of the Mosaic covenant as well as the oral law of the time), non-Jewish peoples who desired to believe in Yeshua were permitted a freedom of choice if they did not wish to observe these features. The primary point is that *Sha'ul* (Paul) did not want the new non-Jewish believers to be caught up in the works of the law as a kind of legalistic service, as if to earn something from God based on self-effort.[4]

But what about the Messianic Jews? When these people—the Nazarenes—were put out of the synagogues, based on Yavneh's decisions, as they left they desired to proclaim to their people, "Yeshua is the Messiah, the atonement for our sins, and he is also deity." David Baron's comment, which Varner notes (page 35), is that worship does not consist in observances but has been replaced by spiritual sacrifices and service that God will honor. But Jewish believers should also be permitted a freedom of choice; and over the next two to three hundred years as they met together to worship, what did they do? They sought to live in accordance with what Yeshua had taught, making use

[4]F. F. Bruce (*Commentary on Galatians*, New International Greek Testament Commentary [Grand Rapids: Eerdmans, 1982], 137–38) points out that "'the works of the law' are not to be deprecated in themselves, for the law of God is 'holy and just and good' (Rom. 7:12). . . . What is deprecated is the performing of them in a spirit of legalism, or with the idea that their performance will win acceptance before God."

of the Mosaic covenant and traditions, as Bellarmino Bagatti and Cardinal Danielou pointed out.[5] Even though the contextualization is now a modified Jewish one, the message is the same: Yeshua is the Messiah and the one who is the only way to God.

But once this body of Messiah became predominantly non-Jewish with a non-Jewish leadership, how did these new leaders solve the problem of the presence of Jewish believers? We already saw the answer in the introduction: The new Jewish believer must give up altogether his or her former identity, become a Christian (that is, a non-Jew, for all practical purposes), forego an entire Jewish background, and adopt the Greek context of proclaiming the faith and living as a believer, in whatever country or culture that might be.

CONCERNS OF DAVID BARON

In his chapter William Varner cites a number of points from a lengthy article of some ninety years ago by the prominent David Baron, who lived in England but who also had a wide ministry in the rest of Europe as well as in North America. The material from Baron's article has become a classic reply in arguments against the existence of the Messianic congregation.

A Messianic Jewish Lifestyle in the Early Church

Baron remarked that within the body of Messiah only one set of rules can exist for the unity between Jews and Gentiles ("neither Jew nor Greek" [Galatians 3:28])—a unity further emphasized in Ephesians 2:11–22, where *Sha'ul* (Paul) states that there is no longer any dividing wall of hostility between Jewish and non-Jewish believers in Yeshua (Ephesians 2:14). Messianic Jews do agree that there is a oneness in the body of the Messiah as each one faces God with no partition. But does this mean we must take away the religious culture and ethnicity of people groups to achieve this unity while living here on earth?

---

[5]See Bagatti, *The Church from the Circumcision;* Jean Cardinal Danielou, *The Theology of Jewish Christianity* (London: Dalton, Longman & Todd, 1964).

The point is that when writing to non-Jewish congregations—in Galatia and Philippi, for example—*Sha'ul* (Paul) gave them a universalistic standing within the body of Messiah, so that non-Jewish believers did not have to follow all that is contained in the Mosaic covenant or the traditions. And when he moved among non-Jewish folks, he may not have made a fuss over his own choices in order to make his non-Jewish contacts feel perfectly at ease. But what did he do on his own as he sought to live as a Messianic Jew? When he showed up in a synagogue on the Sabbath in the areas where he worked, did he not wear some of the traditional garb by which congregational officials would have recognized him as a Jew?[6] Why was he so insistent that, if at all possible, he wanted to be in Jerusalem by the feast of *Shavuot* (Weeks, or Pentecost [Acts 20:16])? Did this holiday have some special significance for him, aside from the anniversary of the coming of the Holy Spirit? And in his letter to the Galatians one finds at least five or six citations or allusions to the Mishnah (the oral law commentary on Scripture).[7]

Furthermore, when the apostles wrote their letter to the congregation in Antioch (Acts 15:22–29), they, too, recognized the principle of universalism that must exist between Jewish and Gentile believers there and allowed for the latter's freedom as well.[8] But what did the apostles have to say to the Jewish believers in the land of Israel? The apostles and their fellow Messianic believers still held to the religious culture of Jewish people in the homeland—that is, that which can be substantiated by a sound biblical theology and specifically by how Yeshua adapted the Mosaic covenant and religious culture of the oral law.

---

[6]As for example, the tallit (prayer shawl).

[7]Galatians 3:15 / *Baba Bathra'* 8:1, in H. Danby, tr. & ed., *The Mishnah* (London: Oxford, 1933), 376; Galatians 3:16 / *Shabbat* 9:2, *The Mishnah*, 108; Galatians 3:16 / Berakoth, 3:3, *The Mishnah*, 4—to mention only a few statements. *Sha'ul* (Paul) sometimes shows how he agrees with the *Mishnah* and at other times he shows how the *Mishnah* differs from the Word.

[8]This congregation may have had an equal number of Jewish and non-Jewish believers. The apostles asked that the latter not eat anything strangled (where blood would have remained entrapped in the animal after its death) and that no blood be used as food, so that their freedom would not be a stumbling block to their Jewish brethren.

A Reply Concerning This Lifestyle

We need to examine at least three areas concerning this Jewish lifestyle as to whether it should continue as *Sha'ul* and other Jewish believers practiced it. Varner points out how *Sha'ul* (Paul) says himself in the plain teaching of Philippians 3:4–8 that the practices of a Torah-observant life are "rubbish." Perhaps, but the emissary may be saying something else as well. Yes, *Sha'ul* had a heritage: his lineage, language, tribal affiliation, and the religious culture of the nation. But Moises Silva points out that "it was not the heritage as such that he revolted against, but the viewing of that heritage as a human right or achievement, thus obscuring one's need for full dependence on God's grace."[9] After this emissary had become a believer he did not feel he had to engage in any self-effort to have a relationship with God: "We have redemption through [Yeshua's] blood, the forgiveness of sins" (Ephesians 1:7); it is "by grace" we are saved, "not by works" (Ephesians 2:8, 9); we receive this "gift of God" which is "eternal life" (Romans 6:23); and so on. But *Sha'ul* continued to live as a Jew among other Jewish believers, as long as that lifestyle was tested by a sound theological understanding and by how Yeshua adapted the oral law.

In a second argument that Jewish believers must give up this Jewish lifestyle, Baron made the point (page 35) that, with the destruction of the second temple, Hebrew Christians were now free of all "national observances"; since the "Jewish national polity" was broken up, believers are no longer dependent on any building or land, and worship does not consist in observances. Granted, the loss of the temple was a trauma for the nation. Many of the leading rabbis were in shock, and the people wrung their hands. One religious leader offered a way out of this predicament, which we shall yet consider.

But what did this mean for Jewish believers in Israel itself? Many would have remembered the words of Yeshua (Matthew 24:2) and possibly would have lamented that the destruction of the temple had to occur. But after having returned from Pella following the revolt, they had a greater task ahead of them in

---

[9]Moises Silva, *Galatians*, The Wycliffe Exegetical Commentary (Chicago: Moody Press, 1988), 180.

reaching out to the people. Quite possibly, because of the reality of having no temple, the believers had the greatest evangelistic outreach ever in the 72 to 100 period. From then on, because of Yavneh's ruling regarding the Nazarenes, some of the believers fell away and gave up on the deity of Messiah, as already mentioned. Others, however (into the 300s and 400s, according to evidence from various sources), lived a lifestyle that reflected the written law and Yeshua's teaching of the New Covenant.

A third area of concern pertains to the "shadows" the Messianic Jew emphasizes through "typical, or symbolic, practices [rather than] emphasizing the 'reality' of New Testament fulfillments" (page 41). Specifically in view are the matters of diet and festival practices (note Colossians 2:16–17; Galatians 4:10; Hebrews 10). Some Jewish believers, because the Mosaic covenant as a package is broken up, feel no obligation to observe the dietary laws or follow the holidays of the Jewish calendar at all. They certainly do have the freedom of choice to live in this manner. But what about those of us who desire to identify ourselves as Messianic Jews and follow the dietary laws and remember the holidays? Do we not have the freedom of choice to do so as well? In the larger body of Messiah I am one with all my fellow Jewish and non-Jewish believers, but in my specific Messianic congregation I have a religious culture I have adopted. Am I living in the "shadows"? When I am in conversation with my people, I emphasize the shadows to demonstrate what God wanted from our people from the beginning. But eventually I also point to the Messiah Yeshua as the fulfillment of these shadows because he is "greater," as the writer of the book of Hebrews affirms to Jewish believers.

In many cases, we as Jewish believers are told to remain Jewish. But at the same time we are also advised to give up our religious culture totally—that is, don't observe the Mosaic Jewish holidays; don't worship on Saturday; don't read the Sabbath portion from the scrolls or comment on it; don't use Jewish prayers of tradition, national rites, or customs. While it is important to train our children and young people in what the Bible teaches and what the Messiah taught, to seek for their decisions for atonement from sin, and to enlist their interest in outreach among all kinds of people, yet we wish to do so in a Jewish cultural context in order that they will know who they are.

AN EXAMPLE OF RELATING TO THE DAY OF ATONEMENT

It would be good to note how the Messianic Jew relates, based on what a good theology offers, to one instance of handling the traditions in his background.

The Background of Atonement from the Oral Law

The modern Day of Atonement liturgy includes the *viddui* (confessions)—a long list of sins to be confessed several times during the course of the twenty-five hour service of fasting and praying. These prayers of confession are at the very heart of repentance for wrongdoing and are a part of what serves as the means for atonement.

This concept traces back to the deliberations by the Council of Yavneh (70–90). These leaders might have thought their decisions would only be in force until a new temple could be built. Perhaps they thought the interval would be as short as the fifty or so years that occurred between the first and second temples. But what they spawned in their directives regarding atonement was an emphasis other than what Moses or any other sacred word from God had ever intended.

At about 200 B.C. Shimon HaZadik (Simon the Just) made a profound biblical observation: "By three things is the world sustained: by the Law, by the Temple-service, and by deeds of loving-kindness."[10] He had encapsulated the biblical message for salvation: the necessity for repentance and prayer, the sin offering and other offerings in the temple, followed by the desire to see genuine followers of the Torah live a godly lifestyle. But at Yavneh in A.D. 73, as the religious leaders heard the desperate cries of other rabbis and the people of the nation, Yohanan ben Zakkai declared to Rabbi Joshua in particular, "My son, be not grieved. We have another atonement as effective as this, and what is it? It is acts of loving-kindness, as it is said, 'For I desire mercy and not sacrifice.'"[11]

[10]*Avot* 1:2 in Danby, *The Mishnah*, 446.

[11]*Avot de Rav Natan*, chapter 4, in Danby, *The Mishnah*, 34.

What ben Zakkai had chosen was only two of Shimon's statements: those regarding repentance and the godly lifestyle, whereby people could have forgiveness of sins. Judaism became a religion with no substitute atonement; salvation was based on self-effort. Ever after Yavneh, when the rabbis speak of salvation we always have to assess specifically what they have in mind: physical, national, spiritual, or whatever else. Atonement now in the Jewish community cannot be regarded in the same way in which Moses had proclaimed it.

A Biblical Offering

Let us take a more in-depth look at one example of what it means to worship in a Messianic Jewish sense, using the best techniques of a biblical theology in a contextualization for worship on the Day of Atonement, the most sacred day on the Jewish calendar.

Do we approach the Day of Atonement exactly as outlined in Leviticus 16 or in *Yoma* in the Mishnah?[12] Not at all, because no temple has existed since A.D. 70, no altar is present, and the priests of Levi cannot minister. We also know what Yohanan ben Zakkai directed for the Day of Atonement worship at the Council of Yavneh apart from temple worship.

What then does the Messianic Jew proclaim? Our task is to share what Moses taught concerning the sin offering. The high priest first offered up a bull on the Day of Atonement (Leviticus 16:11), which was the sin offering for himself and his family. The second set of animals included two goats, the first for the sin offering on behalf of the people of Israel while the second was to picture how God can take away the sin of each Israelite if he will believe in the principles of this offering (Leviticus 16:7–10).

Accompanying the sin offering were the principles pictured in Leviticus 4:27–29 in relation to the offerings for individuals, while the goat sacrifice was the offering for national atonement (Leviticus 16:8). The first principle was substitution. The high priest had to realize this basic truth, but each Israelite

[12]*Yoma*, chapters 5–6, in Danby, *The Mishnah*, 168–69.

also had to accept this guideline. No one could approach God apart from it. The second principle was identification. The high priest placed his hands on the head of the animal and confessed the sins of the people and the goat became identified with the sins of the people.[13] Each Israelite did likewise when he offered his sacrifice, confessing his own sins. Furthermore, the high priest, as well as the Israelite when he offered his animal substitute, had to personally kill the animal. Each animal was identified with the sins of the offerer; the goat of sacrifice carried the sins of the nation, and each Israelite's animal carried the sins of the offerer. For this reason each of the substitutes had to die. But God wanted the offerer in each case to realize this truth because, in actuality, as the high priest stood in place of the people on the Day of Atonement, he killed this animal. And as each Israelite offered his sin offering, he likewise had to understand the penalty of sin and recognize that he was responsible for the death of the substitute; and therefore he had to kill it.

A third principle is also present: the exchange of life. In each case, the substitute had to die because it now carried the sin-life of each party. But when it died, it gave its *own* life to the offerer. By no means was this automatic. Among the people on this sacred day, only those who believed in and accepted these three principles would know finally this new life the Spirit of God would make possible. The individual offering his substitute-sacrifice had to make a personal commitment of belief in these principles if he were also to experience what atonement, or salvation, means. Many did understand this message and knew what it meant for their sins to be removed "as far as the east is from the west" (Psalm 103:12).

The Transfer from Moses to Yeshua

While the Mosaic covenant *as a package* no longer exists, two of the elements of the covenant do: the sacrificial system

[13] Ibid.

and the moral law.[14] Certainly we do not offer sacrifices today, but the sacrificial system of five sacrifices is subsumed in the one offering by the Messiah. The first one to which we must relate, once for all, is the sin offering. Our altar today is the tree or execution-stake on which Yeshua died (Romans 3:25; 1 Peter 2:24), and the priesthood is that of Melchizedek, the one to which the Messiah belonged (Hebrews 7:17). Such is the new covenant message.

In the parallel between the Mosaic covenant and the new covenant, we note how Yeshua is our substitute (John 1:29); he is our identification—when we place our hands on his head and confess our sins, he takes our sins upon himself (1 Corinthians 15:3; 1 Peter 2:24); he died—and it was our sins that caused his death; and finally, when we believe in him, he gives us his life (John 10:10).

What does one do with the long list of prayers for forgiveness in the *siddur*? A biblical salvation is not based on repentance and prayer alone, important as they are. Instead, the Messianic Jew retains and reads these prayers in the Messianic *siddur*, slowly and meaningfully—but not as the means for atonement, or salvation, but rather that we may do what is right in God's sight. These well-crafted prayers become the means by which we keep a close watch on our lives for our sanctification, and they can be adapted to fill a most important need in the lives of believers.

As we explain Moses to our people who will attend our services on this sacred day—the Day of Atonement—we will have presented the essential background given to our people through the covenant of Moses. But as we explain the connection from Moses to Yeshua and the atonement, or salvation, of today, we have a message to give our people from our background concerning the meaning of salvation.

---

[14]From the internal evidence of Leviticus, four elements make up the Mosaic covenant: the moral law of the Ten Commandments; the five Levitical sacrifices (these first two elements are a part of the new covenant as well); the civil and criminal law codes, which do not transfer to the new covenant; and the models of worship (holidays) and lifestyle (dietary codes and a multitude of other guidelines), which, because of a universalism within the body of Messiah, one is free to practice or not practice.

Because we explain the Jewish roots of our faith in Yeshua, does this mean that we now have peace with the Orthodox Jew who practices a strict particularism? Of course not. Messianic Jews seek to make the connection with what Yeshua taught, and so the Orthodox will say that we are no longer Jews—that we have adopted another religion. But some will recognize the Mosaic source of our message and respond to the message and become believers. Our task is to present a biblical message to our brethren, and so we affirm our identity and our peculiar lifestyle to make the shadows live in the reality of Israel's Messiah.

MODERN ASSEMBLIES OF JEWISH YESHUA-BELIEVERS BETWEEN CHURCH AND SYNAGOGUE[1]

An Israeli Response to William Varner

Gershon Nerel

My response to the question "Do we need Messianic congregations?" is to replace the question mark at the end of this phrase with an exclamation mark. We *must* have congregations of Jewish believers in Yeshua! Inherently, it should be noted that any talk about not needing Messianic congregations de facto implies that all the Jews, and among them also Jewish Yeshua-believers, do not need to remain a distinct community. A brief look into historical facts clearly demonstrates that Jewish believers in Yeshua, when requested to find all in all within Gentile churches, eventually lost all Jewish characteristics. History also proves that the initial "entry ticket" of Jewish Yeshua-believers into those churches gradually ended, sooner or later, with a national "exit ticket" from the Jewish commonwealth.

[1]I owe special thanks to the late Haim Joseph (Haimoff) Bar-David, a faithful disciple of Yeshua (1905–1991) and a pioneer in the Land of Israel since the times of the British Mandate. Haimoff/Bar-David, who was proud to be named a *biblical fundamentalist*, persistently provided a living example and encouragement for a new generation of Israeli Yeshua-believers. See Gershon Nerel, "Haim (Haimoff) Bar-David: Restoring Apostolic Authority among Jewish Yeshua-Believers," *Mishkan* 37 (2002): 59–78.

In essence, the leading question that needs to be asked is this: "Why did the Messianic congregations disappear from the historical narrative of the church?" The answer is *not* to be discovered within Holy Scripture but rather in the explanations rooted in the aftermath of the *historical interactions* between Jews and Gentiles. The examination of the "need for Messianic congregations" depends ultimately on searching the historical domain, honestly and unsparingly, and *not* focusing exclusively on the biblical text. The theme of "congregations of Jewish Yeshua-believers" is *not* to be exhausted only within theological speculations but should relate to post-biblical developments realistically affecting Jewish survival.

The New Testament, indeed, nowhere nullifies the rationale for maintaining distinctive assemblies of Jewish believers in Yeshua. At the same time, however, both Gentile and Jewish congregations of believers in Yeshua cannot avoid facing the fervent sparks of the historical and current dissonance between Jews and Gentiles. Specifically, the real question behind the scenes is, "Who should hold the leading spiritual authority?"

As a matter of fact, throughout history Jewish believers in Yeshua faced opposition not only from their brethren within the synagogue but also from their brethren within the church. Sadly, yet all too often, the long-lasting encounters—even confrontations—between Gentile and Jewish believers in Yeshua also reflected struggles about control, human interests around prestige, and particularly about theological hegemony. The question before us is how to bridge the historical gap of the last two millennia in the relations between Jewish and Gentile believers in Yeshua, restoring Jewish congregations in a way that basically resembles the situation in the first century A.D. In order to facilitate the reading of this response, I am going to refer to Jewish believers in Yeshua by the acronym JBY.

WHO IS A HERETIC?

Almost always, church and synagogue placed JBY on the marginal side of esoteric heretics, as opposed to the mainstream nonheretical "orthodox believers."[2] It was particularly within the repeated apologetic debates between church and synagogue that the existence of JBY groupings was negated,[3] and in fact the same way of thinking still affects the contemporary attitude of many churches towards JBY.

Since the early centuries when the "church of the uncircumcision" outnumbered the "church of the circumcision," it became clear that congregations of JBY created a perpetual problem, even a threat, to the mushrooming Gentile churches.[4] Whereas the Gentile Christians acted to stand apart from the synagogue and all the Jews, they also did their utmost to classify "Jewish Christians" under the categories of an old sect or a new cult. Practically, many leaders within both church and synagogue have systematically discredited, disinherited, and delegitimized the survival of independent groupings of Jewish believers in Yeshua.

Paradoxically, on the one hand the majority of the Gentile churches expressed sharp anti-Jewish attitudes toward JBY, while on the other hand they welcomed them with a vast "bear hug." This double-faced approach usually resulted in the assimilation of JBY within the institutional churches and then in the surrounding non-Jewish society. In recent times, however, the phenomenon of corporate and autonomous groupings of JBY has reached a momentous watershed in the course of history.

BACK TO HISTORY

After an absence of about eighteen centuries, various associations of JBY have reappeared within current history. The modern movement of JBY is again taking its place on the stage of history—mainly through the establishment of distinctive congregations and alliances. Alongside the watching eyes of both church

---

[2]See F. Stanley Jones, "Introduction," in Simon C. Mimouni and F. Stanley Jones, eds., *Le Judéo-Christianisme dans tous ses états* (Paris: Les Éditions du Cerf, 2001), 13–14. Cf. Gershon Nerel, "A Marginal Minority Confronting Two Mainstreams: Jewish Followers of Jesus Confronting Judaism and Christianity (1850–1950)," in Shulamit Volkov, ed., *Being Different: Minorities, Aliens and Outsiders in History* (Jerusalem: Shazar Center for Jewish History, 2000), 283–97 (Hebrew).

[3]See Ora Limor, *Jews and Christians in Western Europe: Encounter between Cultures in the Middle Ages and the Renaissance*, vol. 1 (Tel-Aviv, 1993), 68–76 (Hebrew). Cf. Israel Jacob Yuval, *Two Nations in Your Womb: Perceptions of Jews and Christians* (Tel-Aviv, 2000), 26–39, 82–93 (Hebrew).

[4]See James Parkes, *The Conflict of the Church and the Synagogue* (New York: Atheneum, 1974), 92–95.

and synagogue, these corporate entities emphatically embrace the axiom that they are reentering history not merely as legitimate and autonomous entities but also as a fulfillment of biblical prophecy, linked to the national restoration of Israel.

The historical reappearance of modern assemblies of JBY has been a developing process in the last two centuries. In reality this movement progressed side by side with two other occurrences: the activism of millenarian evangelicals on the one hand, and the accomplishments of Herzlian Zionism on the other.[5] Consequently, the unprecedented return of JBY into the historical arena considerably challenges nowadays the historical heritage of both church and synagogue. Especially after the Holocaust and the foundation of the state of Israel, congregations of JBY have stimulated the church to examine its own traditions and norms vis-à-vis its Jewish roots.

At the same time, in fact, modern congregations of JBY do form a fragmented movement, much like the reality within mainstream church and synagogue, yet most JBY share the vision of being no less Jewish than Yeshua himself and his first disciples. Still, many Messianic congregations are strongly influenced by the Gentile churches and their denominational teachings and traditions. However, these influences are not necessarily negative. Thus, for example, when certain Israeli congregations of JBY are singing traditional church hymns and carols translated into poetic Hebrew, they nevertheless *do not* feel that this hymnology is detracting the congregation from Jewish characteristics or Hebraic identity—as long as they introduce fresh insights into biblical exegesis.

Nowadays it occurs in many congregations (and not only in Israel) that JBY are reexamining the traditional definitions concerning Christological formulas and eschatological issues deeply anchored in church history. Thus, in opposition to the traditional creeds of the churches, some JBY reformulate the historical definitions regarding the Trinity and the divinity of

[5]Yaakov Ariel, *Evangelizing the Chosen People* (Chapel Hill, N.C.: University of North Carolina Press, 2000). Cf. Gershon Nerel, *'Messianic Jews' in Eretz-Israel (1917–1967): Trends and Changes in Shaping Self-Identity* (Dissertation, Hebrew University of Jerusalem), 1996.

Yeshua. By doing so, these assemblies endeavor to exclusively focus on biblical vocabulary. For example, certain congregational creeds deliberately omit the term *Shilush* (Trinity), arguing that it is an idolatrous concept of paganism "because it teaches that Yeshua and the Holy Spirit are gods on their own merit," thus originating from "churchianity" and not from the Bible.[6]

Unfortunately, sometimes such theological redefinitions of Christological issues can lead eventually to the total denial of Yeshua's divinity.[7] Yet similar topics certainly shape the congregational agenda of JBY—either openly or covertly.[8] At the same time, one should not automatically conclude that whenever congregations of JBY rephrase the historical creeds about Christology they reject Yeshua's divinity. In fact, most congregations of JBY do believe in Yeshua's full divinity, even when not referring to the historical term *Shilush*.

THE TRAP OF MIXED NOMENCLATURE AND PRAXIS

Groupings of JBY frequently adopt the terms "Messianic Judaism" and "Messianic synagogues" in order to highlight their linkage with mainstream Jewry. At the same time, and almost unanimously, they refrain from using the appellations "church" and "Christian," thus wishing to distance themselves from the *goyim*, the Gentiles, who within Jewish collective consciousness are still expecting their assimilation. Furthermore, together with the appellations of "Messianic Judaism" and "Messianic synagogue," many JBY also endeavor to adopt ceremonial traditions of rabbinical Judaism (for example, men covering their heads, using ritual prayers from the *siddur*, and congregating around folkloristic dance—practices that actually have no biblical foundation).

---

[6]See Tsvi Sadan, "The Trinity—Midrash or Dogma?" *Israel Today* (Jerusalem, November 2001): 20.

[7]See "Messianic Jews Debate the Deity of Jesus," *Israel Today* (Jerusalem, November 2001): 21.

[8]See Gershon Nerel, "Creeds among Jewish Believers in Yeshua between the World Wars," *Mishkan* 34 (2001): 61–79.

In my view, these JBY wrongly assume that with an outward dress of "Jewish nomenclature" and ceremonial symbols they can get the acceptance of mainstream Jewry. As a matter of fact, it was the Israeli Supreme Court that put an official end to such naive hopes. Functioning as the final legal instrument of the Jewish state, the Israeli *Bagatz*—High Court of Justice—has again and again ruled that a Jew, even if observing *all* rabbinical traditions of "Judaism," yet at the same time also believing in Yeshua, is regarded as "a Jew embracing another religion." Consequently, such a person is no longer considered to be a Jew.[9]

Accordingly, a Jew who believes in Yeshua is automatically placed outside the boundaries of normative Judaism, no matter the nomenclature or praxis that he or she adopts. Thus, it is precisely the opposite direction that JBY need to follow. JBY should stand aloof from rabbinical Judaism and challenge its "Jewish" legitimacy and authority—just as Yeshua himself did. In other words, contemporary JBY should redefine authentic Jewishness. Instead of following traditional Judaism or the synagogue, JBY should embrace only solid biblical principles, with no reference whatsoever to the Jewish oral law, the *Halakhah* (rule of conduct), which is still far from being the final authority among all Jewry.

In addition, because Judaism and synagogue continue to maltreat the name of Yeshua and still excommunicate his Jewish disciples,[10] it is not only out of context but even pathetic that congregations of JBY wish to follow rabbinical culture and institutions. Therefore, when JBY confuse their Jewish ethnic and national identity with synagogue patterns of thinking and behavior, they fail to appreciate the centrality of Yeshua and his message. In other words, the "Synagogue JBY" are actually confusing fundamental biblical priorities with attitudes that at best marginalize Yeshua. Thus, in my opinion, when JBY adopt the rabbinical terminology and practice of Judaism and synagogue, they totally lose focus and mislead not merely themselves but many others as well.

---

[9]*Beresford vs. Ministry of Interior Affairs*, Verdict of the Israeli High Court of Justice (file no. 265/87, 25 December 1989 [Hebrew]). Cf. leading case of "Brother Daniel," Oswald Rufeisen, and Benjamin Shalit, in A. F. Landau, ed., *Selected Judgments of the Supreme Court of Israel* (Jerusalem, 1971).

[10]See Yehuda Liebes, "Mazmiah Qeren Yeshu'Ah," *Jerusalem Studies in Jewish Thought* 3 (1983/84): 313–48 (Hebrew).

Moreover, while religion and nationality are inseparable within Jewish tradition, ethnically only one Jewish nation still exists. However, theologically we can easily point to the existence of several "Judaisms."[11] Thus, for example, Rabbinical/Orthodox Judaism differs fundamentally from Secular/Humanistic Judaism.[12] Similarly, substantial differences apply with regard to Reform and Conservative Judaism. Therefore, another focal question today is not about who may belong to Judaism but about what Judaism is. Or, what is the definition for "authoritative Judaism" in light of the diverse "Judaisms" within the Jewish commonwealth? And more specifically, through which of the diverse "Judaisms" can one identify the real Messiah and Redeemer?

Currently this acute problem is dramatically reflected among the Jewish opponents of the "Lubavitcher Messiah," sarcastically criticizing the large *Chabad* movement as "a religion closest to Judaism."[13] Interestingly, the Chabadnic Messianic Jews even attribute divinity to their "Messiah" and expect his resurrection. Nowadays, some other dead and living rabbis within Jewry are emphatically considered by their followers to be *the* Messiah. Among the names we can mention, for example, are the late Rebbe Nachman of Breslav and Rebbe Kook.[14] Furthermore, Israeli assemblies of JBY need to carefully define the use of the term "Messianism," because it is also combined today with territorial aspirations of political right-wingers within Israeli society such as the followers of "Gush Emunim" (Bloc of the Faithful).[15] The complexity of designations, ideologies, and

---

[11]See Amos Mokadi, *The Challenge: A New Jewish Paradigm* (Tel-Aviv, 1997 [Hebrew]).

[12]See Yehoshua Arieli, "On Being a Secular Jew in Israel," *The Jerusalem Quarterly*, 45 (1988): 49–60. Cf. Dedi Zucker, ed., *We the Secular Jews* (Tel-Aviv 1999 [Hebrew]).

[13]See David Berger, "The Rebbe, the Jews, and the Messiah," *Commentary*, vol. 112 (2001): 23–30.

[14]See Seffi Rachlevsky, *Messiah's Donkey* (Tel-Aviv, 1998), 291–93, 365–66 (Hebrew).

[15]See Maurice Bowler, "Chabad, Gush Emunim and Messianism," *The Messianic Jew* 67 (1994), 30–33; Aviezer Ravitzky, *Messianism, Zionism and Jewish Religious Radicalism* (Tel-Aviv, 1993), 111–200 (Hebrew).

actions interrelated within the Messianic domain calls us to carefully define our terminology.

Reasonably, therefore, we should ask this: With which sector of "Messianic Judaism" does JBY wish to be part and parcel? For me this is merely a rhetorical question, since even the term "Messianic" cannot exclusively be applicable as a name for JBY. As a result of the contemporary situation, systematic differentiation must be made between three blurred terms—Judaism, Jewry, and Jewishness—and these specifications are not mere semantic games.

To summarize, therefore, in order to escape an unavoidable conceptual trap, which, in fact, can also lead to confusing the Word of God with human traditions, congregations of JBY should abandon the terms "Messianic Judaism" and "Messianic synagogue." These terms cannot even be optional, as they automatically cause chaotic confusions and misrepresentations. Therefore, I would offer a solution to this trap by simply avoiding any "ism." JBY should only adopt the biblical term *talmidim—disciples—of Yeshua* (Acts 6:1–2; 20:1). This scriptural designation, or simply *ma'aminim be'Yeshua—believers in Yeshua,* immediately calls for orderliness within the polyphonic labyrinth of our times.

CONFRONTING THE CHURCH'S ANTI-JEWISH LEGACY

The "church of the uncircumcision" contributed much to the liquidation of the original JBY and even now attempts to limit the influence of today's congregations of JBY. The church of the Gentiles defined its own identity by expressing contempt toward Jewish characteristics—including JBY. During many centuries the church developed anti-Jewish doctrines and declared that it had replaced the Jews as the real "chosen people."

Historically, the Gentile church fathers not only insisted that JBY must become 100 percent Christians, without any Jewish characteristics whatsoever, but developed strong anti-Jewish exegesis based on a theology of systematic differentiation of the Gentiles from the Jews.[16] Contemporary JBY confront such attitudes

[16]See François Blanchetière, *Enquête sur les racines juives du mouvement chrétien* (Paris, 2001), 507–14.

down to this day because too often the churches want to see JBY as museum exhibits. Many churches view congregations of JBY as associates not to be fully trusted or accepted—those who pose a danger to the Gentile establishment and tradition.

Because the congregations of JBY regard themselves as an integral part of physical Israel, this stands in the way of the self-definition of the Gentile churches as the "true Israel" *(Verus Israel)*.[17] In fact, from the early centuries the church opposed the option of having independent assemblies of JBY, as this remained a standing menace for her own raison d'être, threatening to overthrow Gentile prerogatives of theological leadership and prestige. Thus today many church figures struggle, mostly behind the scenes yet sometimes out in the open, *against* having a "Jewish church," a distinct assembly of JBY, *within* the universal church.[18] Such church leaders simply want JBY to integrate inside the Gentile churches, yet it is a very dangerous decision to remove an independent presence of a Jewish element among the universal body of believers.

As part of its anti-Jewish policy to legally authenticate its own inheritance through the invalidation of Jewish foundations, the church replaced the Jewish calendar with a new one. The change of the biblical lunar calendar, as well as the observance of Sunday, obviously affected not only the keeping of the seventh-day Sabbath but also the biblical Passover, since Easter always had to fall on a Sunday.[19] Hence, when modern congregations of JBY still follow the biblical/Hebraic calendar for their feast celebrations, they are frequently treated by non-Jewish believers as "obsolete workers" who put their hands to the plow and look back (Luke 9:62).[20]

---

[17]See Marcel Simon, *Verus Israel: The Relations between Christians and Jews in the Roman Empire* (Oxford: Oxford University Press, 1996).

[18]See Gershon Nerel, "'Verus Israel'?: Jewish Believers in Jesus—A Challenge for the Church," paper presented at the international conference on The Dynamics of Antisemitism in the Second Half of the Twentieth Century (Jerusalem, 13–16 June 1999).

[19]See Samuele Bacchiocchi, *From Sabbath to Sunday* (Rome: Pontifical Gregorian University Press, 1977), 165–235.

[20]See *Grace and Truth,* Collectio Hebraica Hierosolymitana (Jerusalem, 1948), 82 (Hebrew).

The issue of circumcision provides another example of the church's anti-Jewish attitudes. Throughout the Middle Ages and until recent times, churches required JBY to adopt "professions of faith" by which they had to undertake not only to stop "carnal circumcision" but also to renounce this practice publicly.[21] Historically, the church opposed circumcision among JBY, not merely because it gave no salvation credit, but also because the church refused to tolerate any outwardly Jewish national sign uniquely and perpetually belonging to the seed of Abraham (Genesis 17:1–14). In other words, the change of the calendar and the abolition of circumcision as a national act for JBY were instrumental in the church's triumphalism over the Jews. The established Gentile church deliberately disassociated itself from Jewish/biblical rites—particularly in order to enforce its absolute authority over the *kehilot* (congregations) of JBY.[22] Unfortunately, this is not merely a remote episode.[23]

One observes today as well within the universal body of Yeshua-believers the question, "Who should hold the theological hegemony?" These feelings not only exist but still shape the identity of both Gentile and Jewish believers in Yeshua. But this is mostly an undercover phenomenon, since nowadays it is politically incorrect to pronounce such ideas in the open.[24]

Protestants as well as Catholics refuse to recognize JBY as proper Jews, and therefore demand that they get out of the Jewish community, over and over relying on the misinterpretation of a partial verse—"There is neither Jew nor Greek" (Galatians 3:28). This partial quotation makes use of a third of a biblical verse, ignoring the fact that the quotation also deals with male and female and master and servant, each of whom retain their distinctiveness.

For example, in 1964 the Lutheran World Federation officially declared that the term "Hebrew Christian" (and I would

---

[21]Parkes, *The Conflict of the Church and the Synagogue*, 394–97.

[22]Oded Irshai, "The Church of Jerusalem—from 'The Church of the Circumcision' to 'The Church from the Gentiles,'" in *The History of Jerusalem* (Jerusalem, 1999), 61–114 (Hebrew).

[23]See Melanie Phillips, "Christians Who Hate the Jews," *The Spectator* (16 February 2002).

[24]See Nerel, "Verus Israel?" 15–16 (see http://sicsa.huji.ac.il/absdynam.html).

add how much more the term "Messianic Jew") "introduces unbiblical divisions into the church."[25] This statement inherently was not merely a refutation of terminology relating to individual JBY vis-à-vis the Gentile church, as some had thought.[26] The real fear expressed here was, in fact, of separate and unassimilable "Jewish churches." However, just as there are natural differences between male and female within the church itself, it is natural to distinguish between Jewish and Gentile believers in Yeshua. Within congregations, JBY have a distinct calling and testimony to witness about the Jewish Messiah both for church and synagogue. Obviously, however, while there is no biblical commandment for women to form their own branch within the church, still there exists a clear biblical call for Israel's permanent distinctiveness.

ISRAEL'S IRREVOCABLE ELECTION

Against various aspects of the historic "Replacement Theology" within the churches, the modern congregations of JBY stand today as a living example that God has neither rejected nor forsaken the "apple of his eye," his people Israel (Zechariah 2:8). These assemblies reflect a reality that corresponds to the words of the apostle Paul, who clearly promotes the doctrine of Israel's election *as a nation*: "as far as election is concerned, they [Israel] are loved on account of the patriarchs, for God's gifts and his call are irrevocable" (Romans 11:28–29). Consequently, the modern congregations of JBY, as in the first centuries, represent the unique remnant of Israel "chosen by grace" (Romans 11:5). In other words, this remnant must remain a distinctive body, retaining its unique characteristics within its own congregations and fellowships.

While contemporary assemblies of JBY stand as the "firstfruits" of Israel, they also point to the rest of the nation of Israel as God's elect *(am segula)*, that eventually those living during Messiah's return will be saved in a wonderful way (see Romans

[25] "The Church and the Jewish People," *The Lutheran World*, vol. 11 (1964): 266.

[26] See H. D. Leuner, "Is 'Hebrew Christian' Theologically Correct?" *American Hebrew Christian*, 51 (1966): 3–9.

11:26–27). At the same time, however, the church of the Gentiles cannot take the place of physical Israel by claiming that it is the "true Israel." According to God's perpetual election of Israel as a nation, JBY must also keep their distinctive corporate identity even within the present time frame of the body of Messiah.

It is absolutely true that the non-Jewish believers in Yeshua participate in Israel's spiritual heritage (see Ephesians 1:3–5), yet this universal election does not cancel the particular election of Israel. Israel has to remain separate—as there is an election within an election. Obviously, from the viewpoint of atonement and salvation there is no difference whatsoever between Jew and Gentile, yet from a *functional* perspective, Israel—and within it the assemblies of JBY—has a unique calling. This calling is to remind the Gentiles about their Jewish roots and to interpret Scripture in a new way (for example, to show that *Sha'ul* (Paul) did not betray his people but also stands as a faithful "apostle to the Jews."[27]

THE TIMES AND THE FULLNESS OF THE GENTILES

The restoration of authentic assemblies of JBY is "life from the dead" (Romans 11:15). God works uniquely through such congregations, and we can see that they appear increasingly on the public agenda of both church and synagogue. Likewise, the present territorial restoration of Israel, with Jerusalem as its sovereign capital, is the clear fulfillment of the "dry bones" prophecy, nationally awaiting Israel's spiritual revival (see Ezekiel 36:22–28; 37:1–14). *Medinat Israel*, the state of Israel, poses a great challenge to the *Golah*, the Jewish Diaspora, while Israeli congregations of JBY embody a double challenge—challenging both the Gentile churches and the Jewish assemblies of JBY that wish to remain in the Diaspora. As now "the times of the Gentiles are fulfilled" (Luke 21:24), a new era dawns with the modern congregational movement of JBY.[28]

[27]See Moshe Immanuel Ben-Meir, *How a Jew Explains Ephesians* (Jerusalem, 1978).

[28]See Hubert Panteny, "This Time and Our Task," *Jerusalem*, vol. 62/63 (Nov./Dec. 1951): 6–8.

Nowadays there is much apostasy within the churches, and they desperately need a reformation. Today a variety of unbiblical doctrines anchored in New Age philosophy, in environmental "green theology," in "success theology," and in feminism, as well as in the deification of humanity, to mention only a few, are spreading within numerous churches.[29] These churches must place reformation ahead of revival.[30] This reformation should come not only from within the Gentile churches themselves but also from the assemblies of JBY as they introduce a "Jewish Reformation."

Israel as a nation and particularly the modern congregations of JBY present today a special test for the Gentile churches. The churches must realize that the congregations of JBY have a unique task that only Jews can fulfill. A basic example would be the real, not semantic, shift from "missionizing" to *witnessing* about Yeshua.

NEITHER GENTILIZING NOR JUDAIZING

In the present time, while churches seem willing to welcome the conformist *individual* JBY, most of them repudiate such *corporate* entities. This is especially true when the Gentile churches view the congregations of JBY as nonconformist and "schismatic" dissidents. History has shown that the greatest wrong of the churches has been the Gentilizing of JBY, despite what is being said to the contrary.[31] Following historical precedents, many Gentile churches still turn a deaf ear to the biblical truth that the non-Jewish believers in Yeshua "do not support the root, but the root supports [them]" (Romans 11:18). As the wild olive shoot is grafted into the cultivated olive tree and *not* vice versa (see Romans 11:17–24), the Gentile churches should naturally acknowledge the distinctive assemblies of JBY.

Congregations of JBY should maintain their Jewish identity, yet by all means they should not seek to Judaize the Christians

---

[29]See Hank Hanegraaff, *Christianity in Crisis* (Eugene, Ore.: Harvest House, 1993).

[30]See Dave Hunt, *Beyond Seduction: A Return to Biblical Christianity* (Eugene, Ore.: Harvest House, 1987), 29–43.

[31]See M. J. Levy, "To Atone for Christendom's Greatest Wrong to the Jews," *Hebrew Christian* 1 (1929): 194.

from the nations. Conversion to "Judaism" by circumcision or any other external practices should be fully rejected. Similarly, JBY should not be Gentilized by denying their right to corporately observe the God-given—not rabbinical—customs of the Jewish people. In such a congregational way JBY remain loyal to national Israel, thus giving a sense of natural belonging and self-confidence within the same family—and the Gentile churches should sympathetically support this.

Congregations of JBY should definitely not be comprised exclusively of Jews, yet those non-Jews who join them should come with the attitude of Ruth the Moabitess, and they should be accepted and welcomed as she was. The entire mixed congregation should still maintain a biblical Jewish—not rabbinical—identity. This can be best accomplished in the Jewish state, not in the Diaspora, as JBY become immersed in a Jewish culture and naturally practice the Jewish calendar and holy days in workplaces and schools. Only in Eretz-Israel (the land of Israel) can assemblies of JBY maintain a Hebraic identity together with non-Jewish believers—without Gentilizing or Judaizing each other.

EPILOGUE

Any study concerning the legitimacy and authority of modern congregations of Jewish believers in Yeshua should focus on the *combination* of biblical verses and the historical developments of the last two millennia. Historically, both church and synagogue shaped their own identity by neutralizing the distinctiveness of corporate entities of JBY. Even today, in fact, the very existence of independent congregations of JBY is still provoking both Jewry and Christendom. Recently, however, while more churches manifest growing interest in their Jewish roots, they are also willing to admit the church's wrongdoing against JBY and repent.[32]

Nowadays, it is through their congregations, not only as individuals, that JBY are influencing bit by bit both mundane and sacred history. They are back in the historical arena in order

---

[32]See, for example, Peter Hocken, *The Glory and the Shame: Reflections on the 20th-Century Outpouring of the Holy Spirit* (Guildford, England: Eagle, 1994).

to fulfill a significant role within the eschatological developments still expected to take place. Modern assemblies of JBY are no longer an episodic "nonissue" that can be simply ignored.

Therefore, on the basis of historical experience, one may expect that, without the existence of autonomous and viable assemblies of JBY, the beliefs of the Gentile church are constantly liable to the danger of relapsing into neo-paganism. It is no secret that those churches that have distanced themselves from Jewish-biblical components have also retreated from the Word of God. Humanistic compromises and liberalism have deeply penetrated the church. Nonbiblical doctrines and cultic theology control many aspects of church life. The parallel congregations of JBY with their Hebraic teaching of Scripture can be an inducement to return to the plain meaning of Scripture. Congregations of JBY have the task of a corporate watchman, warning and challenging both church and synagogue according to the fundamental teachings of the Bible.

The very fact that *congregations of JBY lack a two-millennia tradition* helps them to easily find the bridge between themselves and the first-century model of JBY as portrayed in the New Testament. In fact, modern congregations of JBY fully credit the Gentile church for the preservation and the canonization of the New Testament and accept the scriptural canon as a fait accompli.[33] Congregations of JBY, as self-governing entities, accept the canonical text and the guidance of the Holy Spirit for their spiritual legitimacy and authority. Even without the historical continuity of a formal apostolic succession, congregations of JBY are *not* an anachronism. In reality these congregations form a tangible bridgehead with the Jewish assemblies of the early centuries.[34]

In the opening years of the twenty-first century, the existing "church market," either on the Protestant or the Catholic and Eastern Orthodox side, can hardly offer an alternate authentic place for the autonomous congregations of JBY. Even having

[33]See Gershon Nerel, "The Authoritative Bible and Jewish Believers," *Messianic Jewish Life* 73 (2000): 16–19.

[34]See Daniel C. Juster, "The Government Question for the Messianic Congregations," *Kesher* 10 (2000): 46–47.

fully authoritative assemblies of JBY *within* the church establishment is not realistic. Rather, as free and self-governing entities, loyal to both King Messiah and the nation of Israel, congregations of JBY should exist *alongside* the Gentile church; and as two autonomous brotherly bodies within the body of Messiah they can fruitfully influence each other. Cooperation will come more readily with the churches among the nations, and so Yeshua will really appear as *Ahinu* (our brother) and the best friend of the Jews.[35]

[35]See Evert van der Poll, *De Messiaanse Beweging* (Putten, Netherlands: Shalom Books, 2001), 291–308.

Chapter Two

MESSIANIC CONGREGATIONS MAY EXIST WITHIN THE BODY OF MESSIAH, AS LONG AS THEY DON'T FUNCTION CONTRARY TO THE NEW TESTAMENT

Arnold G. Fruchtenbaum

MESSIANIC CONGREGATIONS MAY EXIST WITHIN THE BODY OF MESSIAH, AS LONG AS THEY DON'T FUNCTION CONTRARY TO THE NEW TESTAMENT

Arnold G. Fruchtenbaum

I take as my starting point in this chapter the fact that Jewish believers in the messiahship of Yeshua are still Jews. They do not cease to be Jews by becoming believers in Yeshua. The writings of the New Testament show that, even after faith, Jewish believers are referred to as Jews, and Gentile believers are referred to as Gentiles. Hence, the new faith does not change one's ethnic identity (see Romans 11:11–24). Furthermore, Jewish believers have a dual citizenship in that they are part of the remnant of Israel and they are the Jewish wing of the church. Being part of the Jewish wing of the church means that all believers, both Jew and Gentile, make up the same body—the body of the Messiah (see Ephesians 2:11–3:6). On the other hand, Jewish believers also make up the present-day remnant of Israel (see Romans 11:5–6), and the remnant is always part of the nation and not detached from the nation. Thus, there is a distinctive Jewish identity in the body of the Messiah.

THREE BASIC QUESTIONS

If the question is asked, "Are Messianic congregations a biblical necessity or requirement?" then the answer has to be no.

The Bible does not require uniquely Jewish congregations for Messianic Jews any more than it requires other ethnic churches, such as Black churches, Latino churches, Chinese churches, or others.

If the question is asked differently, "Is it biblically permissible to have Messianic Jewish congregations?" then the answer is yes. Jewish believers have the right to set up uniquely ethnic Jewish congregations that reflect the Jewish culture and style of music, worship, teaching, and so on, just as Black, Latino, and Chinese churches would reflect their particular style of worship and culture. In other words, this is a biblically neutral issue, which means that the Lord has given us freedom in these areas. Our congregations are not required to follow a certain type of structure and culture. Therefore, there is no reason to assume (as some have) that, while all other ethnic groups may have their own ethnic churches, Messianic Jews are forbidden to do so.

If yet a third question is asked, "Is it mandatory for Jewish believers to attend only Messianic Jewish congregations?" again the answer is no. What is so beautiful about being a believer in the Messiah and about the grace that comes with it is the absolute freedom to be part of any body of believers who share the same faith. A Jewish believer has the full freedom to be part of a Messianic congregation, and he also has the freedom to join a church that may be totally (or almost totally) Gentile in its membership and outlook. The final criterion cannot be whether something is Jewish or not, but rather whether what is being taught lines up with the Scriptures. I direct a ministry that has planted or co-planted Messianic congregations in six different countries. However, I see many Messianic congregations whose doctrinal position I question and whose worship style allows all kinds of "wild things" to occur—and there is nothing Jewish about them. I have often directed Jewish believers to go to a sound Bible-teaching and Bible-believing church rather than a Messianic congregation infested with questionable teachings.

As I write this chapter, the reader should be aware that I am in favor of Messianic congregations and am a member of one, but I do not necessarily see Messianic congregations being the final answer or the best solution for all Jewish believers everywhere.

THE PROBLEMS OF JEWISH BELIEVERS IN RELATION TO THE LOCAL CHURCH

Problems on the Side of the Local Church

First of all, the local church today is a Gentile-cultured church and feels quite foreign to most Jews. It is a culture from which a Jew shies away, not necessarily because he feels that the Jewish culture is superior but simply because the Gentile culture is strange. This does not mean that the influence of Gentile culture is biblically wrong; it simply means that it is not Jewish.

Anti-Jewishness is a second problem in many local churches. Such a church may extend a Jewish believer membership but will not make him feel welcome, demanding that he give up everything Jewish.

A third difficulty is insensitivity to the needs of the Jewish believers. A Jewish believer faces certain identity problems that the Gentile Christian never has to face. This insensitivity is usually the result of ignorance and misunderstanding rather than of deliberate neglect, but it has driven many Jewish believers out of local congregations.

Fourth, while pro-Jewishness is a good thing in itself, it can also be a problem. Often a Jewish believer is so fussed over that it appears God must expend more energy and grace to save a Jew than a Gentile! Some Jewish believers revel in all this attention and really eat it up. But for others it is strange and unnatural and makes them shy away from the local church.

Problems on the Side of the Jewish Believer

One major difficulty for the Jewish believer is the fear of losing his Jewish identity. Since his own culture is rich with heritage and history, he naturally does not wish to lose it. If he does not fear for himself, he will often fear for his children, who are not likely to be taught any Jewish culture or history in the church education ministries. To drown their Jewishness in the sea of Gentile culture is not something Jewish believers want to happen, and often this is used as an excuse not to join the local church.

A second problem is legalism. Some evangelicals, especially in the United States, have developed extensive "laws" that make activities such as dancing, drinking wine, and watching movies into sin. Although not biblical, these rules have become so engraved into the local church as to make them seem equally inspired with the Ten Commandments and the Sermon on the Mount. To make a sin of dancing and of drinking wine, both strong elements in the Jewish culture, and then to tell the Jewish believer that he must give them up, will often turn him away. Since the Bible does not condemn these things, though the local church does, this inconsistency causes many Jewish believers to avoid the local church.

A third problem is the Jewish believer's desire to continue practicing certain celebrations of Judaism, such as the Passover, and to give his children a Jewish education. It is not possible to do this in most local churches, and so this may also become a barrier to the Jewish believer's uniting with a local church.

A BIBLICAL SOLUTION

The Local Church

The biblical pattern for the local church is pictured in Ephesians 2:11–22. Granted, Paul is mainly talking about the invisible church; yet it does reflect that the pattern for the visible church should be one of Jews and Gentiles forming one body in Messiah. The visible church is comprised of a body of professing and baptized believers united for the purpose of worship, practice of the ordinances, and carrying out of the Great Commission. This body of believers is to contain both Jews and Gentiles. Thus the teaching of Scripture is against both total isolation from the local church and separation by forming strictly Jewish congregations where Gentile membership is discouraged or sharply limited. The local church must be composed, where possible, of both Jewish and Gentile believers working together for the cause of Messiah. It is to the praise of most Messianic Jews that they have chosen to follow this course and not either of the two extremes.

The Jewish-Oriented Local Church

But what about the problem of retaining Jewish identity? Of raising children in the Jewish culture? Of practicing Jewish festivals? As has been shown, it is not biblical to form a local church composed only of Jewish believers. A biblical option is the planting of a local church with its style of worship and other church-related activities based on Jewish culture and practice. This factor renders it a Messianic congregation. Membership and leadership are open to Jews and Gentiles alike, but Gentiles who join would favor this Jewish orientation of the local church. This approach has the advantages of meeting all the Jewish needs of Jewish believers described earlier. The rest of this chapter will expound on this option.

THE FOUNDATIONS OF MESSIANIC CONGREGATIONS

One apologetic for Messianic congregations has been that this would be the best way to reach out to the unbelieving Jewish community. However, after twenty-five years of existence, this has not proven to be the case. Most Jewish members of Messianic congregations (and often the Jewish members are in the minority) did not come to the Messiah through the witness of a Messianic congregation but became part of one only after becoming believers. The majority came to the Lord through the witness of Jewish missions such as Ariel Ministries, Chosen People Ministries, or Jews for Jesus, among others, or were witnessed to by Gentile believers totally outside of a Messianic context and not necessarily in a Jewish way.

For me, this is not a negative. Nor is it an issue, for while I believe that one purpose of a Messianic congregation is to reach out to the Jewish community in a Jewish context, I do not see this as the primary purpose for having a Messianic congregation. The primary purpose should not be for the sake of the unbelieving Jewish community but for the sake of the Messianic Jewish community. In other words, the main purpose is for the benefit of Jewish believers—to meet the needs and the desires of Jewish believers and to provide Jewish believers with a Messianic community where they are comfortable in expressing their Jewishness. This community enables parents to instill Jewish continuity in their children as they learn the meaning of both Jewishness and faith in the Messiah Yeshua, and are able to express both aspects in one basic culture—a Messianic Jewish culture.

Thus it is irrelevant whether the larger Jewish community accepts us as Jews or not, because we do not exist to impress them with our Jewishness and our Jewish loyalties. We do this for our own benefit; we do this for ourselves because this is who and what we are. However, it is important that such practices rest on a solid biblical and theological foundation.

As the doctrine of the remnant of Israel teaches, there always were, are, and will be Jews who believe and make up "the Israel of God" (Galatians 6:16). The remnant of Israel today are the Jewish believers in the messiahship of Jesus. Throughout history since Jesus, there always were Jewish believers in Yeshua, and periodically in certain parts of the world there were sudden increases in the number of Jewish believers. It is not the purpose of this section to discuss the various segments of the movement but to defend biblically the right to its Jewish identity and the right to express its Jewishness as a distinct entity within the body of Messiah, the church.

Based on what has been said, let us take a look at four important propositions with regard to Messianic Jewish practice.

The Role of the Mosaic Law

First, *Messianic Jewish practice cannot be based on the law of Moses as an obligation, for the law has been rendered inoperative and is no longer in effect.* The emphasis of this proposition is on the word "obligation." It would be biblically wrong to impose the law of Moses as a rule of life on the Jewish believer. The clear-cut teaching of the New Testament is that the law of Moses has been rendered inoperative with the death of Messiah. In other words, the law in its totality no longer has authority over any individual.

This is evident first of all from Romans 7:1–6. When a husband dies, his wife becomes a widow and thus is no longer bound to "the law of marriage" (verses 1–3). Therefore, she is free to remarry without committing the sin of adultery; she is now "released from the law" because a death has taken place. Paul then makes the theological application (verses 4–6). Here, again, a death has taken place, the death of the Messiah. Believers have "died to the law through the body of Christ" (verse 4). The sinful nature can no longer use the law as a base of operation (verse 5).

Finally, Paul states that "we have been released from the law" (verse 6). One is either married to the law or to the Messiah but cannot be married to both.

Then, secondly, Paul adds in Romans 10:4: "Christ is the end of the law so that there may be righteousness for everyone who believes." The Greek word *telos* ("end") can mean either "termination" or "goal." However, as all Greek lexicons show, the evidence clearly favors the meaning of "termination" or "end." For example, Thayer gives the primary meaning of *telos* as "end, i.e., a termination, the limit at which a thing ceases to be, ... in the Scriptures also of a temporal end; ... Christ has brought the law to an end."[1]

Not only does Thayer give "termination" as the primary meaning of *telos*, he also includes Romans 10:4 as belonging to this category of usage. Nor is "goal" listed as a second or even a third priority of usage; it is fourth on the list. Arndt and Gingrich give the primary meaning of the verbal form as "bring to an end, finish, complete."[2] The nominal *telos* is given the primary meaning of: "End ... In the sense of *termination, cessation.*"[3] They list Romans 10:4 as being in this category, and list the meaning of "goal" as third in priority. For the Jewish believer especially, the law of Moses has been rendered inoperative, since Gentiles were never under it to begin with. Furthermore, Romans 10:4 should also be interpreted within the wider context of Romans, which includes what Paul wrote in 7:1–6 when he declared that we are "released from the law." Consistency in interpreting Romans indicates that 10:4 must mean "termination" and not "goal."

Third, the law was never meant to be a permanent administration but a temporary one, as evidenced in Galatians 3:19: "What, then, was the purpose of the law? It was added because of transgressions until the Seed to whom the promise referred had come." In context, Paul stated that the law of Moses was an addition to the Abrahamic covenant (verses 15–18). It was added for the purpose of making sin very clear so that all will know

---

[1]Joseph Henry Thayer, *Thayer's Greek-English Lexicon of the New Testament* (Grand Rapids: Zondervan, 1963), 619–20.

[2]W. F. Arndt and F. W. Gingrich, *A Greek-English Lexicon of the New Testament and Other Early Christian Literature* (Chicago: University of Chicago Press, 1957), 818.

[3]Ibid., 819.

that they have fallen short of God's standard for righteousness. It was a temporary addition until the "Seed" (Messiah) would come; now that he has come, the law is finished. The addition has ceased to function with the cross.

The fourth line of evidence is based on Galatians 3:23–4:7. In this passage, the law is looked on as a pedagogue or a tutor over a minor to bring him to mature faith in the Messiah (3:24). Having become believers, we are no longer under this tutor, i.e., the law of Moses (3:25). As clearly as could be stated, this passage teaches that with Messiah's coming the law is no longer in effect.

Fifth, with Messiah there is a new priesthood according to the order of Melchizedek, not according to the order of Aaron. According to Hebrews 7:11–19 the law of Moses provided the basis for the Levitical priesthood, and there was an inseparable connection between the law of Moses and the Levitical priesthood. One could not function apart from the other. The Mosaic law only allowed the Levitical priesthood. For the Levitical priesthood to be replaced by the priesthood of Melchizedek required a change of the law. Was there a change of the law? Hebrews 7:18 states that the Mosaic law was "set aside" in favor of a new law, which is the basis for the priesthood according to the order of Melchizedek. In other words, if the Mosaic law were still in force, Yeshua could not be our high priest since he was of the tribe of Judah, and "in regard to that tribe Moses said nothing about priests" (verse 14).

Sixth, the law was the dividing wall of hostility that has now been broken down, according to Ephesians 2:14–15. The Mosaic law served as a dividing wall to keep the Gentiles from enjoying the spiritual blessings of the Jewish covenants. If the Mosaic law were still in effect, it would still be a wall to keep the Gentiles away—but that wall was broken down with the death of Messiah.

The seventh line of evidence for the annulment of the Mosaic law, 2 Corinthians 3:1–11, zeros right in on the part of the law that most people want to retain, namely, the Ten Commandments. In verse 7 it is called the "ministry that brought death"; in verse 9 it is called the "ministry that condemns." In verses 3 and 7 the spotlight is on the Ten Commandments, since it is these that were "engraved in letters on stones." The main point then is that the law of Moses, especially as represented by the Ten Commandments, is a *ministry that brought death and condemnation.* If the Ten Commandments were still in force today, this would still be true. However, they are no longer in force, for Paul states in verses 7 and 11 that the law has faded away. The Greek word used is *katargeō,* which means "to render inoperative." Since the emphasis in this passage is on the Ten Commandments, this means that the Ten Commandments have been rendered inoperative.

To summarize, the law is a unit comprised of 613 commandments, and all of it has been rendered inoperative. It is no longer the rule of life for Jewish believers.

A favorite objection to the above view of the law of Moses is Messiah's statement in Matthew 5:17–18. Messianic Jews who cite this passage are seldom consistent on this. It is obvious that Yeshua was speaking of the law of Moses. Yet no Messianic Jew who claims to be "Torah observant" accepts his own thesis since he must believe in the doing away with, in some form, of many of the commandments of the law of Moses, if not most. The commandments concerning priesthood and sacrifice are only one example, and others can be cited. Regardless of the semantics used to describe this change ("superseded," "brought to greater fulfillment," "bringing out its true meaning," and so forth), it is clear that a great many of the 613 commandments no longer apply as they were written. Yet Matthew 5:19 adds "the least of these commandments," which emphasize the entire law—all 613 commandments.

True, Yeshua did come to fulfill the law; but the law of Moses did not end with the coming of the Messiah or by his life, but by his death. As long as he was alive, he was under the Mosaic law and had to fulfill and obey every commandment applicable to him. The statement of Matthew 5:17–19 (verse 19 must not be ignored) was made while he was living, and as long as he was living he had to obey the law of Moses in every commandment in the manner Moses commanded and not in the way the rabbis had reinterpreted it. Even while he was living, he already implied the doing away of the law. One example is Mark 7:19: "In saying this Jesus declared all foods 'clean.'" Again, all must admit that great parts of the law no longer apply in the manner prescribed by Moses. Have they been done away with or not? To constantly claim that the law of Moses is still in effect or that it is the same as the law of Messiah, while ignoring the details of that same law, is inconsistent and a theological fallacy.

Those who argue for a mandatory observance of the law of Moses will often refer to Exodus 31:12–17: to verse 13, which states that the Sabbath is to be observed "for the generations to come"; to verse 16, which says that the Sabbath is to be a "lasting covenant"; and to verse 17, where the Sabbath is to be a sign between God and Israel "forever." According to the proponents of mandatory Sabbath keeping, these terms show that the Sabbath obligation continues, although many other parts of the Mosaic law are no longer in effect, such as the sacrificial system and the Levitical priesthood. However, while the English terms do tend to carry concepts of eternity, this is not the meaning of the Hebrew words themselves. Classical Hebrew had no word that actually meant "eternal." The Hebrew term for "forever" *(olam)* means "long duration," "antiquity," or "futurity."[4] The Hebrew terms basically mean "until the end of a period of time." What that period of time is must be determined by the context or by related passages. The period of time may have been to the end of a man's life, or an age, or dispensation, but not "forever" in the sense of eternity. This is very clear from examining the usage of the same terminology in other passages.

For example, the same Hebrew term for "forever" is used to mean nothing more than up to the end of a man's life in Exodus 21:6; Leviticus 25:46; Deuteronomy 15:17; 1 Samuel 1:22; 20:23; 27:12; and 1 Chronicles 28:4. Another way the same term was used was when God said that he would dwell in the Solomonic temple "forever" in 1 Kings 9:3 and 2 Chronicles 7:16. However, God left the temple in the days of Ezekiel. Obviously, "forever" here meant the age or period of time of the first temple only.

Even more relevant to the issue at hand is that this same term was applied to facets of the law of Moses that Messianic Jews teach are no longer in force, such as the kindling of the tabernacle lampstands (Exodus 27:21; Leviticus 24:3); the ceremony of

---

[4]Francis Brown, S. R. Driver, and Charles A. Briggs, *A Hebrew and English Lexicon of the Old Testament* (Oxford: Clarendon Press, 1907), 761.

showbread (Leviticus 24:8); the service of the brazen laver (Exodus 30:18); the Levitical priesthood and the priestly garments (Exodus 28:43; 40:15; Leviticus 10:9; Numbers 10:8; 18:23; 25:13; 1 Chronicles 15:2; 23:13); the sacrificial system, including sacrifices and offerings (Exodus 29:28; Leviticus 7:34, 36; 10:15; Numbers 15:15; 18:8, 11, 19; 19:10); and the Yom Kippur sacrifice (Leviticus 16:34). If it is insisted that the Sabbath is still mandatory on the basis of the English word "forever," then the same thing would have to apply to all these other facets of the law of Moses. Yet those who insist on mandatory Sabbath keeping often insist that the Messiah has put an end to all the others.

As for the term "lasting covenant," it is also used of the ceremony of the showbread in Leviticus 24:8. And as for the term "for the generations to come," this, too, is limited in time. It is used of the Levitical priesthood (Leviticus 10:9; Numbers 18:23), the ceremony of the lampstands (Exodus 27:21; Leviticus 24:3), the service of the brazen laver (Exodus 30:21), and the sacrificial system (Leviticus 7:36; Numbers 15:15).

It is inconsistent exegesis to insist on the basis of such terms as "forever," "for the generations to come," and "lasting covenant" that the Sabbath and festival law is still mandatory without incorporating all of these other elements from the law of Moses for the same reason.

The law of Moses has been disannulled and we are now under a new law. This new law is called the law of Messiah in Galatians 6:2 and the law of the Spirit of life in Romans 8:2. This is a brand-new law, totally separate from the law of Moses. The law of Messiah consists of all the individual commandments from Yeshua and the apostles applicable to the New Testament believer. A simple comparison of the details will show that it is not and cannot be the same as the law of Moses.

Two observations are worth noting. First, many commandments are the same as those of the law of Moses. For example, nine of the Ten Commandments are also in the law of Messiah. But, second, many are different from the law of Moses. For example, there is no Sabbath law now (Romans 14:5; Colossians 2:16) and no dietary code (Mark 7:19; Romans 14:20).

The reason there is so much confusion over the relationship of the law of Moses and the law of Messiah is that many commandments are similar to those found in the Mosaic law, and many have concluded that certain sections of the law have, therefore, been retained. It has already been shown that this cannot be the case, and the explanation for the sameness of the commandments is to be found elsewhere. The explanation can best be understood if it is realized that there are a number of law codes in the Bible, such as the Edenic, Adamic, Noahic, Mosaic, New, and Kingdom. A new code may contain some of the same commandments of the previous code, but this does not mean that the previous code is still in effect.

While certain of the commandments of the Adamic code were also found in the Edenic code, it did not mean that the Edenic code was still partially in force; it ceased to function with the fall of man. The same is true when we compare the law of Messiah with the law of Moses. The law of Moses has been rendered inoperative and we are now under the law of Messiah. There are many different commandments and also many similar commandments, but they are nonetheless in two separate systems. If we do not kill or steal today, it is not because of the law of Moses but because of the law of Messiah. On the other hand, if I steal, I am not guilty of breaking the law of Moses but of breaking the law of Messiah.

The believer in Messiah is free from the law of Moses. This means that he is free from the necessity of keeping any commandment of that system. On the other hand, he is also free to keep parts of the law of Moses that do not violate the law of Messiah if he so desires. The biblical basis for this freedom to keep the law can be seen in the actions of Paul, the greatest exponent of freedom from the law. His vow in Acts 18:18 is based on Numbers 6:2, 5, 9, and 18. His desire to be in Jerusalem for Pentecost in Acts 20:16 is based on Deuteronomy 16:16. The strongest passage is Acts 21:17–26, where we see Paul himself—the apostle of freedom from the law—keeping the law. The believer is free from the law, but he is also free to keep parts of it.

Thus, the Jewish believer has the freedom to obey certain commands that are New Testament-neutral, meaning they do not violate any New Testament principle or command. The Jewish believer does *not* have the freedom to choose to obey many of the commandments, such as sacrificing for sin, for that would violate clear New Testament truths, such as Hebrews 10:18. However, many of the commandments, such as keeping the

Sabbath or the dietary rules, would not violate any New Testament imperative, and so there is freedom in these choices.

A recent and strong trend in the Messianic movement is that of "Torah observance." Adherents of this trend *do* see the law as an obligation, and they have, in fact, been splitting Messianic congregations in many different places. It has been my observation that many in the "Torah observant movement" are not even Jews but Gentiles—the kind of Gentiles to whom Paul's letter to the Galatians was written. Because the Messianic movement has not been clear on the role of the Mosaic law in the life of the believer, it is now in turmoil over this very issue. The fact is that leaders have failed to show where the line is to be drawn. With no real parameters, and since it is obvious that no one is really "Torah observant" in the way Moses prescribed, this has led to a great disagreement as to what degree of Torah observance Messianic Jews should be obligated to keep. Some are more extreme than others in causing these unnecessary divisions, but to a great degree the leaders of the movement must take the blame for being so confused about the role of the law.

The simple fact is this: Regardless of whether they claim to be "Torah positive" or "Torah observant," no one really keeps the Torah the way Moses actually required it to be kept. Even the most zealous "Torah observant" Messianic Jews, while teaching law, are actually practicing grace. For example, they would require Messianic Jews to keep the Passover. On what basis must we keep the Passover? Their answer is, because Moses said so. What else did Moses say? For one thing, he said that Passover is not to be observed at home, but "in the place [God] will choose as a dwelling for his Name" (Deuteronomy 16:6), which ultimately became Jerusalem. If there is any Messianic Jew who celebrates either Passover or Weeks or Tabernacles at home or in the country where he lives and does not travel three times a year to Jerusalem, he is not observing the Torah but is practicing grace. Grace permits a Messianic Jew to observe Passover anywhere.

Furthermore, at every Messianic Jewish *seder* I have ever attended (except my own) the main course was roasted chicken. But what does the Torah require as the main course for Passover? Roasted lamb. This is what I serve in my own *seder* at home. Messianic Jews choose to serve chicken because this is what Ashkenazi rabbis required.[5] This is *not* being Torah observant. Once again, they are preaching law while practicing grace, because grace allows you to serve any type of meat at Passover.

Another example has to do with the proper way of observing the Sabbath. Most Messianic Jews are under the misconception that the Sabbath was observed as a mandatory corporate day of worship. Actually, Moses commanded the Jews to stay home and observe the Sabbath as a day of rest rather than a day of corporate worship. Sabbath corporate worship was mandated for the priesthood in the tabernacle/temple compound but not for individual Jews elsewhere. So if a Messianic Jew gets into his car, starts the engine, and drives to his congregation on Friday night or Saturday morning, he is actually breaking the Sabbath in the way Moses prescribed it. Once again, he is preaching law while practicing grace. Grace permits one to stay home and rest on the Sabbath, it permits one to have corporate worship on the Sabbath, it permits one to have corporate worship on any other day of the week.

In my many discussions with and observations of those who claim to be either "Torah positive" or "Torah observant," they are not really and truly observing Torah in the way Moses commanded. Their lives are simply full of inconsistencies and contradictions along this line.

Here is a simple, yet biblical, solution. The Bible teaches that the Mosaic law has been rendered inoperative as an obligation on Jewish believers. As stated earlier, this frees the Jewish believer not to observe these commandments since he is now under the law of Messiah, but on the other hand he is free to observe those commandments that are New Testament-neutral and do not violate any commandment of the law of Messiah. (For example, the law of Moses forbade a Gentile to be invited to one's Passover unless he was circumcised first; the law of Messiah would forbid requiring that obligation on the Gentiles before they can sit at our Passover table.) Furthermore, the Messianic Jew is not only free to observe those commandments of the law of Moses that are New Testament-neutral, he can observe them in

[5]Ashkenazi Jews are historically Yiddish-speaking European Jews who settled in central and northern Europe, or their descendants.

a variety of different ways: He can obey them Mosaically, i.e., the way Moses actually prescribed, or he can observe them rabbinically, or he can combine mixtures of both. On the other hand, he must not judge the Jewish loyalties or Jewish identity of other Jewish believers who may choose to follow these laws differently or not follow them at all.

The Role of Rabbinic Judaism

The second proposition regarding Messianic Jewish practice is that it cannot be based on rabbinic Judaism as an obligation. Again, the emphasis is on the word "obligation." Modern Judaism can be defined simply as the religion of many Jews; it is no longer safe to say "most Jews." Jewishness itself cannot be defined on the basis of religion.

There is an abundance of beauty in Judaism, and Messianic Jews value and appreciate much of it and the part it has played in Jewish history. Nevertheless, they recognize its failure to see Messianic fulfillment in Yeshua of Nazareth. Modern Judaism has many practices, rules, and beliefs that are not found in Scripture but have developed in the course of history through rabbinic and talmudic traditions. These have equal authority in the eyes of Orthodox Judaism. Since the Bible must be the only source of authority for Jewish believers, they reject these practices as binding and obligatory and are free from any need of observing them. However, just as freedom from the law means freedom also to keep certain aspects of the law, so freedom from Judaism also frees the Messianic Jew to keep certain aspects of Judaism that do not violate the law of Messiah, such as the Jewish holy days.

The Role of Ritual Observances

The third proposition concerning Messianic Jewish practice is that there are certain advantages for a Messianic Jew or a congregation to keep some or all of the feasts and to practice other rituals of Judaism. First and foremost, these practices provide a good opportunity for the Jewish believer to express and identify with his Jewishness and the Jewish people. This matter of identification is very important as a testimony to the Jewishness of the faith. Second, they provide a basis for teaching Jewish culture and history. This is especially important for instilling Jewishness in the children of Messianic Jews. Third, they provide opportunities to worship God, both individually and corporately, and to thank him for what he has done in the course of Jewish history and for what he has done for us in the Messiah's fulfillment of the Jewish holy days. Fourth, they provide good opportunities to share the faith with unbelieving Jewish people, showing how the particular feast points to the messiahship of Jesus. Fifth, they provide the Jewish believer with a means of practicing his Jewishness. Regardless of the rabbinic additions, these practices are more biblically based than many practices associated with Christmas and Easter.

However, there is a danger that must be avoided. Jewish believers cannot celebrate these holy days and other Judaistic practices in strict accordance with Judaism. While they are free to copy those things from Judaism that do not go against Scripture, they are not free to use those that do. Many of the services of Judaism cannot be used in their entirety since there are sections that clearly go against the teaching of the New Testament. The prayer book for *Yom Kippur* and the *Haggadah* for Passover are examples of this. For example, the *Yom Kippur* prayer book contains prayers asking God for atonement, but for Messianic Jews, the atonement is in the finished work of the Messiah on the cross, and for those who believe, it is a past act and a present reality. Hence, in our Messianic congregation, the *Yom Kippur* service is a thanksgiving service to express gratitude that we have already received atonement and the forgiveness of sins. As for the *Haggadah,* a number of the blessings refer to things God was said to have commanded but never did, and therefore these blessings will need to be reworded or rewritten.

Another example arises from the observance of Sabbath by lighting the candles. This practice was never commanded in the law of Moses but is of rabbinic origin. However, since it is not forbidden by the New Testament, it is biblically neutral. The Jewish believer is free to kindle the Sabbath lights, but he is also free not to. However, the prayer that goes with it states: "Blessed are You, O Lord our God, King of the universe, Who has sanctified us with His commandments and commanded us to kindle the Sabbath candles." The truth is that no such command "to kindle the Sabbath candles" is found anywhere in Scripture. This prayer is not biblically neutral, and a Jewish believer would be wrong to recite this prayer. The believer, then, has three options. First, he may choose to dispense with the prayer altogether. Second, he can reword the prayer to bring it into conformity with biblical truth. The last phrase could read "*permitted* us to kindle the Sabbath candles." Third, he may choose to make up his own prayer. For my home, I have the blessing recited as follows: "Blessed are You, O Lord our God, King of the universe, Who has sanctified us by his grace and has permitted us to kindle the Sabbath candles and has given us Yeshua the Messiah, the Light of the World, to enlighten our paths." Messianic Jews are free to participate in these kinds of things, but the guiding principle is that of conformity with the Scriptures and their faith in Jesus the Messiah.

The Application to the Messianic Congregation

The fourth proposition regarding Messianic Jewish practice is that, since Jewish believers have a great deal of freedom in living a Jewish lifestyle (as other ethnic peoples are free to live their cultural lifestyle), they have the right to develop Messianic Jewish congregations so that the style of worship and music has a Jewish cultural orientation rather than a Gentile one. Like any other New Testament-based congregation, it must have open membership to any of "like faith," regardless of national, ethnic, or racial background. Neither membership nor leadership can be limited to Jews only, for that would violate biblical truth. Like individual Jewish lifestyles, the congregational Jewish lifestyle, format, and practice must also conform to New Testament truth and must take priority over rabbinic traditions.

Furthermore, even the Messianic Jewish congregations must view themselves biblically, which means they must recognize themselves to be a local church and part of the universal church, the body of Messiah, and not part of Judaism. This does not mean that a Messianic congregation must use the word "church" in its name. In light of the negative connotations the term has developed in the Jewish community because of what has happened in Jewish history, it would be unwise for this word to be used. But Messianic believers must not deny what they are biblically. The issue here is what this congregation is, biblically speaking—and biblically speaking, it is a church.

CONCLUSION

I find myself very comfortable in my Messianic congregation in Orange County, California, because of the measure of freedom allowed to individual members. If you attended one of our *Shabbat* services, you would find some men wearing *kippot*, while others do not. Some of the men wear *tallitot*, and others do not. Some women have their heads covered in accordance with their understanding of 1 Corinthians 11, and other women do not. There is no peer group pressure for anyone to conform to a certain style of Jewish terminology or Jewish dress. No one has a fit if the term "Jesus" or "Jehovah" is used. To me this is a sign of maturity, for I view squabbles over terminology and what I would call "Messianic political correctness" as a sign of immaturity. There are far more important theological issues facing the Messianic movement today than to worry about how a specific name of the Father or the Son or the Spirit should be pronounced.

MESSIANIC CONGREGATIONS SHOULD EXIST AND SHOULD BE VERY JEWISH

A Response to Arnold Fruchtenbaum

John Fischer

Arnold Fruchtenbaum perceptively and cogently begins his chapter this way (page 111):

> I take as my starting point in this chapter the fact that Jewish believers in the messiahship of Yeshua are still Jews. They do not cease to be Jews by becoming believers in Yeshua. The writings of the New Testament show that, even after faith, Jewish believers are referred to as Jews, and Gentile believers are referred to as Gentiles. Hence, the new faith does not change one's ethnic identity (see Romans 11:11–24).

Fruchtenbaum's understanding is not only biblical, but it is also fundamental to the issue at hand. And from this well-laid foundation he correctly derives this principle (page 112): "Jewish believers have the right to set up uniquely ethnic Jewish congregations that reflect the Jewish culture and style of music, worship, teaching, and so on, just as Black, Latino, and Chinese churches would reflect their particular style of worship and culture." And while it may not be "mandatory" for Messianic Jews to attend Messianic congregations, as Fruchtenbaum rightly notes, it certainly seems both beneficial and important. In fact, one may even say that Messianic congregations are the *optimal* solution for Jewish believers for the *very* reasons he puts forward in favor of such congregations as a *possible* solution.

THE PROBLEMS OF JEWISH BELIEVERS IN RELATION TO THE LOCAL CHURCH

Fruchtenbaum rightly recognizes the problems resident in many churches. From a Jewish vantage point, the culture of the church is quite foreign and very un-Jewish. Far too frequently, there is even residual anti-Jewishness found there as well, from the expectation of ceasing the practice of Jewish identity to attitudes more virulent. In addition, often the lack of awareness of and sensitivity to specifically Jewish concerns and circumstances hampers those in churches from effectively assisting and encouraging Messianic Jews as they seek to develop their relationships with God. As Fruchtenbaum astutely points out (page 115), Messianic congregations benefit these believers and meet important needs. And perhaps even more important, these congregations "provide Jewish believers with a Messianic community where they are comfortable in expressing their Jewishness . . . [and in being able] to instill Jewish continuity in their children." Add to this the factor that others in the Jewish community, including family members, tend to be more open to visiting Messianic congregations than churches, and a strong case emerges for such congregations serving as a best-case scenario for Messianic Jews.

THE ROLE OF THE LAW

While for Fruchtenbaum clearly "the law of Moses has been rendered inoperative with the death of Messiah" (page 116), others do not see this issue as quite so "clear-cut." The numerous discussions surrounding this topic in *Kesher* (the journal of the Union of Messianic Jewish Congregations) and elsewhere[1] serve as but one indicator of the differences of opinion on this matter.

[1]For example, see Joseph Shulam, "The Halachic Process," *Kesher* (Summer 1997); John Fischer, "Would Yeshua Support Halacha?" *Kesher* (Summer 1997); David Friedman, *They Loved the Torah* (Baltimore, Md.: Lederer, 2001); and Ariel and Devorah Berkowitz, *Torah Rediscovered* (Littleton, Colo.: First Fruits of Zion, 1996).

Nor are the citations from Romans (7:1–6 and 10:4) decisive for the position of the abrogation of the Torah. For example, in Romans 7, contextually, the death that has taken place for the believer is with respect to the sinful nature (verses 5 and 6), *not* with respect to the Torah. The description in verse 6, "dying to what once bound us," is a direct reference back to verse 5, "we were controlled by the sinful nature." Thus the believer died to the sinful nature, not the law. And the "law" central to this text is the law of marriage, not the law of Moses. Paul expressly says (in verse 2) that upon the husband's death the wife "is released from the *law of marriage*."[2]

Additionally, the discussion of *telos* in Romans 10:4 seems skewed. Actually, the standard Greek lexicon (Arndt and Gingrich) lists this passage under their category of the use of *telos* as "goal" rather than as "termination."[3] Therefore, the Messiah is the goal of the Torah, not its end; and the Torah then serves as the continuing path leading believers onward to Yeshua. Further, consistency with the context of Romans 10 demands that verse 4 indeed be understood in this fashion. The descriptions of the "righteousness that is by faith" and the "word of faith" in verses 6–8 are in fact quotations of the law itself (Deuteronomy 30:12–14). So the Torah includes both of these essential elements that Romans 10 indicates are an important part of God's *present* plan for the world. This clearly points to the significant continuation of the Torah rather than to its present termination.

The argument of Galatians 3 also does not demonstrate that "the law is no longer in effect" (page 118). Its usage of the image of tutor or pedagogue (Galatians 3:24) is by no means novel. The rabbis of classic Judaism used this same metaphor as well (Pirke Avot 6.3), and they certainly did not argue for the abrogation of the Torah by such usage.[4] In addition, the principle cited in Gala-

---

[2]For a more complete treatment, see John Fischer, "Law in Romans: An Interpretive Proposal," a paper presented for the annual convention of the Evangelical Theological Society, Orlando, Florida, November 1998; available from Menorah Ministries, Palm Harbor, Florida.

[3]W. F. Arndt and F. W. Gingrich, *A Greek-English Lexicon of the New Testament and Other Early Christian Literature* (Chicago: University of Chicago Press, 1957), 818–19.

tians 3:15 (that later covenants do not set aside previous ones), when applied to the Mosaic and new covenants, would also argue for the continuation of the Torah. By that principle the later new covenant does not invalidate the earlier Mosaic covenant.[5] And this is consistent with the renewal procedures and perspectives of the ancient Near Eastern covenants. When a covenant was renewed, the earlier version was not scrapped; it was enhanced and supplemented.[6]

Much the same point is addressed in Hebrews, as Westcott aptly notes:

> Prominence is assigned in the epistle to the Old Testament, both to the writing and to the institutions which it hallows. There is not the least disparagement of the one or the other. From first to last it is maintained that God spoke to the fathers in the prophets. The message through the Son takes up and crowns all that has gone before.[7]

Hebrews, when viewed through this lens, also does not set aside the Torah; it elevates it. And Jeremiah 33:14–26 confirms this. As part of this significant new covenant context (Jeremiah 31–33), this text speaks of God's covenant with the priests enduring forever (verses 17–22). As Fruchtenbaum has noted, "There was an inseparable connection between the law of Moses and the Levitical priesthood" (page 118). Therefore, Jeremiah teaches that the new covenant ratifies the Mosaic covenant; it does *not* replace it.

FULFILLMENT AND "FOREVER"

Fruchtenbaum's attempt to minimize or counter the relevance of Matthew 5:17–20 results in a rather strained argument. Whether Messianic Jews "are seldom consistent on this" (page

---

[4]See Solomon Schechter, *Aspects of Rabbinic Theology* (New York: Schocken, 1961), 136.

[5]For a more complete treatment, see John Fischer, *The Millennial Paradox: Jesus and Judaism* (Baltimore, Md.: Lederer, forthcoming).

[6]See Meredith Kline, *The Structure of Biblical Authority* (Grand Rapids: Eerdmans, 1972), 9–14.

[7]B. F. Westcott, *The Epistle to the Hebrews* (Grand Rapids: Eerdmans, 1970), lviii.; also see the discussion in John Fischer, *The Enduring Paradox: Exploratory Essays in Messianic Judaism* (Baltimore, Md.: Lederer, 2000), 37–60.

119) is really irrelevant to the discussion. The text is quite clear. Yeshua clearly states twice in the same verse (verse 17) that he has not come to abolish the law. Messianic Jewish consistency with regard to Yeshua's teachings is certainly *not* determinative of its validity. If the believers' consistency of practice were the standard of a teaching's relevance, most of the Scriptures would thereby be deemed irrelevant.

Fruchtenbaum then argues that "the law of Moses did not end with the coming of the Messiah or by his life, but by his death" (page 119). This strains the interpretation even further, implying that somehow Yeshua's death was disconnected from his "coming," which is hardly a logical disjunction. (See, for example, Mark 10:45.) Besides, Yeshua did stress, *after* his death and resurrection, that his followers were to teach their disciples *everything* he had taught them (see Matthew 28:18–20). Matthew 5:17–20 would surely qualify as part of that "everything."

Then to state that "even while he was living, he already implied the doing away of the law" (page 119) suggests that Yeshua himself was inconsistent with his own teachings. And Mark 7:19 is by no means an example of this implied "doing away," as the King James Version makes abundantly clear. It quite correctly reads, "goeth out into the draught, purging all meats," rather than "declared all foods clean," as some translations have interpreted the passage. Further, the fact that some details of the Torah cannot later, or today, be carried out is no indication that the law has been done away with. Ezekiel and Ezra certainly would not have argued so for their time, even though an essential part of the Torah—the sacrifices—had been circumstantially suspended. Dr. H. Bruce Stokes, a Christian scholar and professor, has cogently summarized this situation:

> Because no part of the Law shall end until all of it is fulfilled (Matthew 5), my view is that the period we are in has both the former and new covenants operating. The former Mosaic Law, moral and ritual, will continue in part or in whole until the Kingdom established by the Messiah is fully realized.
>
> The sacrificial system ebbs and flows with the availability of a Temple, not a dispensational period. I believe that many of the Torah's commands are situational. When the situation requires, they are not completed (lamb for

Passover). But this does not invalidate them. When the circumstances change (a temple is rebuilt), the requirements remain valid. I don't believe the death of Yeshua changed any of that.

So we have the Torah in full force for Israel and the New Covenant emerging for all peoples, to the Jew first and also to the nations. And the emergence of the New Covenant signals the near (as the second coming is near) completion of the purpose of Torah. But I think it is faulty Christian thinking to assume that the Cross ended any part of the Torah. There is no such statement in the Scriptures.[8]

Fruchtenbaum's treatment of *olam* (Hebrew, "forever"), in order to set aside the plain meaning of Exodus 31:13–17 ("a sign between me and the Israelites forever"), is even more problematic. Genesis 17:7–8, in words that echo Exodus 31, gives the clear sense of the continuous duration of *olam:*

> I will establish my covenant as an everlasting covenant between me and you and your descendants after you for the generations to come, to be your God and the God of your descendants after you. The whole land of Canaan, where you are now an alien, I will give as an everlasting possession to you and your descendants after you; and I will be their God.

This description of the Abrahamic covenant as *b'rit olam* (everlasting covenant) is paralleled by similar descriptions of the Davidic (Isaiah 55:3) and new (Jeremiah 32:40) covenants, as well as God's covenant with Phinehas and the priests (Numbers 25:12–13), which of course is integrally connected with the Mosaic covenant. The *b'rit olam* terminology climaxes in the description found in Ezekiel 37:24–28:

> My servant David will be king over them, and they will all have one shepherd. They will follow my laws and be careful to keep my

[8]E-mail posting to the Union of Messianic Jewish Congregations' leaders' onelist (5 May 2000).

> decrees. They will live in the land I gave to my servant Jacob, the land where your fathers lived. They and their children and their children's children will live there forever, and David my servant will be their prince forever. I will make a covenant of peace with them; it will be an everlasting covenant. I will establish them and increase their numbers, and I will put my sanctuary among them forever. My dwelling place will be with them; I will be their God, and they will be my people. Then the nations will know that I the LORD make Israel holy, when my sanctuary is among them forever.

All these passages indicate that the sense of *b'rit olam* spans the sweep of time. But perhaps Psalm 89:28–29, 35–37 gives the most graphic functional, or descriptive, definition of this significant phrase:

> I will maintain my love to him forever, and my covenant with him will never fail. I will establish his line forever, his throne as long as the heavens endure.... Once for all, I have sworn by my holiness—and I will not lie to David—that his line will continue forever and his throne endure before like the sun; it will be established forever like the moon, the faithful witness in the sky.

Clearly when God describes a covenant in *b'rit olam* or related language, he intends that covenant to last for the life of the universe. This description is consistent with that found in the "new covenant" passage of Jeremiah 33:20–21, where God confirms that, as long as day and night endure, his covenant promises endure. Even the passages cited by Fruchtenbaum to indicate that *olam* applies merely for the lifetime of the person addressed reinforce the aforementioned understanding. *Olam* does connote a *lifetime,* but in the case of the covenants it is not only for the *lifetime* of a person but for the *lifetime* of the nation Israel and the *lifetime* of the universe itself.[9]

THE LAW OF MOSES AND THE LAW OF MESSIAH

Fruchtenbaum's characterization of the law of Moses and its distinctions from the "law of Messiah" are problematic as well. To argue that the Sabbath has been abolished by the coming of Yeshua, as many in fact do, contradicts not only Yeshua's own words in Matthew 5:17–20, as previously noted, but also Paul's statement in Romans 3:31 that faith by no means nullifies the law. It also overlooks Yeshua's statement that those undergoing the troubling events he predicted in Matthew 24 should pray that their flight to escape not occur on the Sabbath (verse 20). If the Sabbath has been set aside, there is no reason to pray in this fashion. And to argue that there is "no dietary code" any longer, based on Mark 7:19, is incorrect, as has already been mentioned.

It is interesting to note that the believer is "free to keep parts of the law of Moses that do not violate the law of Messiah if he so desires" (page 122). The question arises: Which parts of the law of Moses violate the law of the very Messiah who said he would not set aside even the least important parts of that same law of Moses (see Matthew 5:17–19)? And when Paul the apostle and rabbi claimed that he had not violated the laws of the Jews or the laws of the temple—let alone those of Caesar (see Acts 25:8)—which parts of that Mosaic law did he silently, and therefore deceptively, exclude from his testimony here because he had not observed them, since they supposedly "violated the law of Messiah"? Or for that matter, did he deliberately deceive the Sanhedrin when he proclaimed that they could testify to the fact that he had been living

---

[9]For an excellent discussion of *olam*, see David Friedman, "The Relationship of Yeshua and the First Century C.E. Messianic Jewish Community to the Mitzvot of the Mosaic Covenant," unpublished doctoral dissertation, California Graduate School of Theology (May 1992).

"according to the strictest sect of our religion" (Acts 26:5)?[10] His continued consistent observance is further reinforced by his statement to the Jewish religious leadership of Rome in Acts 28:17 that he has "done nothing against our people or against the customs [traditions] of our ancestors."

Further, the Mosaic covenant material is just that—a covenant-treaty, as numerous scholars have demonstrated.[11] It is structured very similarly to ancient Near Eastern treaties of the second millennium B.C., and thus functions very much like them. This function is quite different from that of the ancient law codes, which is the category Fruchtenbaum treats the Torah as being a part of. Theologically, the ancient covenants worked more like documents of grace and love rather than instruments of law. In fact, Deuteronomy 7:12 even calls the Torah a "covenant of love," as does Nehemiah 9:32. The graciousness of God spills out from the very first words of the condensed form of the covenant: "I am the LORD your God, who brought you out of Egypt, out of the land of slavery" (Exodus 20:2). This becomes the first "commandment" according to the classic Jewish perspective, and rightly so, and it is replete with grace. The covenant understanding gets reinforced later in what the rabbis describe as God's thirteen attributes of mercy: "God, compassionate and gracious, slow to anger, abundant in kindness . . . preserver of kindness for thousands of generations, forgiver of iniquity . . ." (Exodus 34:6–7, Artscroll Stone Edition).

It is certainly true that significant parts of "the Messianic movement [have] not been clear on the role of the Mosaic law in

---

[10]In the context here, *ezēsa* ("have lived") likely is a gnomic aorist, or "aorist present," which "expresses general truths"; see A. T. Robertson, *A Grammar of the Greek New Testament in the Light of Historical Research* (Nashville: Broadman, 1934), 836. It is further paralleled by the *present* participle used in Galatians 1:14 to describe Paul's ongoing zealotry "for the traditions of my fathers." This is reinforced by the statements of Acts 25:8 and 28:17, whereby Paul characterizes his own devout observant practice of the Jewish traditions.

[11]For a more complete treatment of the ramifications of a covenant perspective of the Torah, see Kenneth Kitchen, *Ancient Orient and Old Testament* (Chicago: InterVarsity Press, 1968); Samuel Schultz, *The Prophets Speak* (New York: Harper & Row, 1968); Kline, *The Structure of Biblical Authority*; and Fischer, *The Enduring Paradox*.

the life of the believer" (page 123). However, a substantial part of the leadership *has* begun to wrestle with these issues. But then again, these very same "theological-applicational" issues have been discussed and debated by rabbis and believers alike through the centuries: Just how does the divine Torah—written in the time of our ancestors—apply to the present circumstances? The critique of Messianic Jewish practice—that even the self-described Torah-observant people do not keep the Torah as Moses delivered—is therefore misplaced. No Christians—including Dr. Fruchtenbaum, one would assume—keep the New Testament as written. For example, how many believers "greet one another with a holy kiss" (1 Corinthians 16:20) or use matza and wine for communion? Just as for the ancient rabbis these kinds of issues were discussions of *halakhah* (biblical behavioral norms) and application, so also they are for believers today. As for the critique that the Sabbath is a day of rest, not a day of corporate worship, it is both unjustified and anachronistic. Exodus 20:10, by noting that this day is "a Sabbath to the LORD," clearly implies the notion of response and therefore worship, an idea also suggested by Isaiah 58:13–14 ("if you call the Sabbath a delight and the LORD's holy day honorable, and if you honor it by not going your own way ..."). Further, by the time of the second temple the Sabbath clearly was a day of corporate worship, and one in which both Yeshua (Matthew 9:35; Luke 4:16–30) and Paul (Acts 17:2) regularly participated.

CONCLUDING OBSERVATIONS

In conclusion, a few cursory observations are called for. The treatment of the biblical appropriateness—or lack thereof—of Gentile conversion to Judaism deserves discussion, and it does receive one elsewhere.[12] To imply that the traditional Hebrew blessing that reads "Blessed are you, O Lord our God, King of the Universe, who has sanctified us with His commandments ..." is "not biblically neutral" (pages 126–27) does

[12]See Dan Cohn-Sherbok, ed., *Voices of Messianic Judaism: Confronting Critical Issues Facing a Maturing Movement* (Baltimore, Md.: Lederer, 2001).

injustice to biblical truth. In John 17:17, Yeshua prays in a similar fashion: "Sanctify them by the truth; your word is truth."

Fruchtenbaum's discussion of the role of ritual observances and its advantages (pages 125–27) is perceptive and very much to the point. There is much value and benefit here. And his suggestion to highlight the Messianic nature of the Jewish traditions and practices, and especially the holidays, is essential. In fact, this has already been done in a number of cases. There are good Messianic books on the holidays;[13] and there are helpful Messianic guides to the Sabbath worship and traditions (the *siddur*) and to the worship and observance of the holidays (the *mahzor* and festival *siddur*)[14] that feature Yeshua the Jewish Messiah.

Fruchtenbaum notes in a profound comment: "There is an abundance of beauty in Judaism, and Messianic Jews value and appreciate much of it and the part it has played in Jewish history" (page 125). He is absolutely on target, and so underscores the vital significance and contribution of Messianic congregations.

---

[13]See, for example, Barney Kasdan, *God's Appointed Times* (Baltimore, Md.: Lederer, 1996); John Fischer, *The Meaning and Importance of the Jewish Holidays* (Palm Harbor, Fla.: Menorah Ministries, 1979).

[14]See, for example, John Fischer, *Siddur for Messianic Jews* (Palm Harbor, Fla.: Menorah Ministries, 1988, 2002); John Fischer, *Messianic Services for the Festivals and Holy Days* (Palm Harbor, Fla.: Menorah Ministries, 1992).

TESTING HOW JEWISH WE SHOULD BE

A Response to Arnold Fruchtenbaum

Louis Goldberg

A lot of discussion takes place these days among Messianic leaders about being "authentically Jewish." When I first heard the phrase, I presumed it meant Orthodox. How much of the Orthodox practice of tradition do we need in order to be regarded as "authentically Jewish"? And who will we impress? The Orthodox? The Conservative? As soon as we add the proclamation of Yeshua as the Messiah, no matter how much of tradition we observe, we will be considered heretics—or worse, non-Jews! And when anyone takes the view that Yeshua is only the son of God, a created being—or goes even further to declare man is born with the *yeser hara* (the evil inclination), i.e., not having a sinful nature, and at his *bar misvah* he then receives the *yeser hatov* (the good inclination)—they have transgressed the even more important phrases "authentically biblical" and "authentically Yeshua."

As noted in my response to William Varner, most missiologists today not only allow but insist that believers within each cultural expression have the right to contextualize their faith and lifestyle in accordance with their cultural background, as long as no basic Bible doctrine or teaching of Yeshua is either broken or twisted.

What does this mean for Jewish believers? We do affirm we are a part of the body of Messiah. We do not seek to create any dividing wall of hostility. But the cultural context of Yeshua and his followers was Jewish. They were Jewish people. The Messiah reflected in his teaching the context in which he and his followers lived. That is also why *Sha'ul* (Paul) referred to himself as an Israeli (Romans 11:1) and a Jew (Acts 22:3). But affirming an identity is not only the result of ancestry or language. A religious culture arising from the oral law is also a part of who we, as Messianic Jews, are as well. We also must note that the synagogue of the first century was different from what it is today. Our task is to ascertain how much of this tradition we can, or should, appropriate today.

MODERN MESSIANIC CONGREGATIONS

The twentieth century has seen a rise to prominence of the Messianic congregation, initially through the labors of Joseph Rabinowitz in Moldavia, beginning in the 1890s. The counterculture years of 1969 to 1972 saw a great number of young Jewish people come to the Lord and acknowledge Yeshua as the Messiah. While some of these new believers found fellowship in traditional Christian churches, the rest, because of their desire for a clearer Jewish expression of faith in Yeshua, wanted to participate in a witness more culturally attuned to their needs as Jewish people. So these people and their leaders structured Messianic Jewish congregations for their own personal worship, and, through it, as a means to reach out to their kinsmen. The term "Messianic Jew" may have been borrowed from Jewish believers in Israel, who have used it since the 1930s.[1] Today Messianic congregations exist in North America, in the state of Israel, and in countries of Western and Eastern Europe, South America, and South Africa. Messianic Jews are also present in Australia and New Zealand.

---

[1]In the Israeli dictionary, *Even Shoshan*, the term "Messianic Jew" refers to one who is a loyal citizen of Israel, fights in the wars to defend the nation when necessary, and whose faith is in Yeshua the Messiah. When I first visited Israel in 1968, I wrote an article for *Moody Monthly* on the various religious expressions in the state, and I included a description of the Jewish believers in Yeshua in their congregations; "Messianic Jews" was the phrase I used to describe them.

Some Messianic congregations have done well in reaching out to Jewish people, and others, because of strong opposition from their kinsmen or because of mistakes by an untrained leadership, have not. And yet the congregations have provided the opportunity to remind their Jewish members, and others in the Jewish community, that Yeshua the Messiah is a part of their Jewish heritage but that he is also a special person with a distinct message. Messianic congregations do not consist of Jewish believers entirely. Many non-Jewish believers do desire the Messianic worship pattern, recognizing that a certain worship preceded that found in the typical church today; they wish to assert a genuine love for Jewish people and to be in fellowship with them. This kind of congregation also provides Gentile believers a way to bring Jewish friends into a more natural cultural setting where they can seek answers to life, consider the claims of Yeshua, and hopefully make a decision to accept the Messiah.

THE ORAL LAW TRADITIONS

Before I comment on Fruchtenbaum's assertions regarding the Messianic congregation, some observations need to be made on what Yeshua and later Jewish leaders did with the oral law traditions so as to discover how this religious culture can be used for today. Messianic Jewish believers have identified three principles in relation to the oral law: (1) some of it can definitely be used; (2) some of it can be adapted for use; (3) using it indiscriminately is unwarranted.

Some of the Oral Law Can Be Used

Hillel's and Ishmael's rules of hermeneutics,[2] as well as the first three guidelines of *pardes*,[3] all enable one to reflect and interpret a good part of the oral law. Many rabbis had keen insights

---

[2]See Louis Jacobs, "Hermeneutics," in *Encyclopedia Judaica*, vol. 8 (Jerusalem: Keter, 1972), 367–70.

[3]That is, *peshat* (the literal interpretation of a passage from Scripture), *remez* (the use of allusion to explain Scripture), and *derash* (the literal interpretation of several passages of Scripture).

in their interpretation of the written law. For example, when commenting on the despicable sin of slander (Leviticus 19:16: "Do not go about spreading slander among your people"), the suggestion was that "Slander is the third tongue and with it three people are killed."[4]

In another setting, the rabbis once discussed the phenomenon of the red string fastened to the wall of the temple on the Day of Atonement and later to the horns of the scapegoat. The understanding was that if God accepted the atoning sacrifice on this day, the red string would turn white; if not, the string remained red. After the rabbis turned to discuss other issues, one came back to make a very pointed statement: "For forty years before the [second] temple was lost, the red string never turned white again!"[5] The destruction of the temple took place in A.D. 70. What may have transpired forty years prior to this date that prompted Rabbi Nahman ben Isaac to say that God never again accepted the atonement sacrifice? Was he a believer? He doesn't say; nevertheless, it was a cryptic remark to convey a particular message.

Another lesson in morals is similar to what Yeshua himself taught about not judging others (see Matthew 7:1–5). The rabbis also chided the faithful, saying that if one asked his neighbor to remove the splinter from his eye, he could respond, "First take the beam from thine own."[6] In another parallel, an honorable person should make sure that his word is, "Let your 'Yes' be 'Yes,' and your 'No,' 'No'" (Matthew 5:37).[7] Yeshua borrowed from Jewish traditional teaching on many occasions, which may account for the parallels, but it may also have been the case that some of Yeshua's teaching made its way into the oral law at a later date.

Can we use the oral law in our teaching and practice? The guidelines for its usage are clear enough. As long as biblical

---

[4]*Arachin* 15b, in *Kodashin* III, *The Babylonian Talmud*, Leo Jung, ed., (London: Soncino, 1948), 89.

[5]*Rosh HaShanah* 31b, in *Moed* IV, *The Babylonian Talmud*, M. Simon, ed. (London: Soncino, 1938).

[6]*Baba Bathra* 15b, in *Nezikin* II, *The Babylonian Talmud*, M. Simon, ed. (London: Soncino, 1935), 291.

[7]*Baba Metzia* 49a, *Nezikin* I, *The Babylonian Talmud*, H. Friedman, ed. (London: Soncino, 1935), 291.

support for it is present, from either the written law or the New Covenant or both, *if* Yeshua said nothing against it, and if it does not violate a basic neutrality between Scripture and the function of everyday life, it is appropriate to use the traditions. We then need to relate these practices to Yeshua so that we are enabled to grow into his full stature.

Some of the Oral Law Can Be Adapted

Yeshua himself demonstrated how the *seder* services of the Mishnaic observance of the *Pesach* (Passover) can be adapted by introducing the special use of *massah* after the lamb meat of the meal. No mention is made of the special use of such a plate with three pieces of *massah* in the service of that day, although enough *massah* was present on the table for everyone.

Normally the procedure was to go from the meat to the third cup in following the instructions in both the Mishnah and Gemara on this passage. Yeshua, however, added the use of the bread of celebration in the Passover *seder* of his day, thereby providing for his disciples a special application of how he will bear our sins in his own body (see Matthew 26:26). To this day, Jewish and Gentile believers remember in the *se'udat haadon* (Communion service) Yeshua's adaptation concerning the bread and the special message of his atonement for our sins.

Yeshua also spoke of the third cup as the cup of redemption, which is a reminder, for the believer as well as for Israel, of the national deliverance from Egypt (see Exodus 6:6). But he also added to its significance the element of personal redemption because he is our atonement, declaring, "This is my blood of the covenant, which is poured out for many for the forgiveness of sins" (Matthew 26:28).

The rest of the holidays were also adapted to demonstrate the uniqueness of Yeshua the Messiah and Redeemer. On the last and greatest day of the *Sukkot* (Feast of Tabernacles), after priests had obtained water from the pool of Siloam, one of them ascended the altar with both wine and water, pouring it out, and as he did so everyone present began singing a number of psalms, including Isaiah 12:2–3. In the midst of the loud, joyful singing, Yeshua cried out to the crowd, declaring to every worshiper that they were in reality singing of him. If they would believe in him, "streams of living water will flow from within [them]" (John 7:37–38; cf. Isaiah 12:3)! What a drama that must have been. And so adaptations can be made in many areas of the oral law to make it conform to both the written law and the New Covenant.

A wealth of references exist in the Jewish literature that can be used and adapted to sustain a biblical position: the exegesis of a Rashi; the poetry of a Gevirol and HaLevi; essays and homilies by various rabbis; short stories with a strong moral barb from Ashkenazi, Sephardi, and Oriental sources. And it would be a pity to ignore what can undergird one's use of a lifetime of supplements to biblical preaching and teaching.

The Oral Law Cannot Be Used Indiscriminately

Some teaching in the oral law cannot be supported by the written law, the New Covenant, or the teachings of Yeshua. Messianic Jews must remember that whatever application to doctrine or lifestyle is made from the traditional materials must always be under the guidance of revealed truth.

Yeshua himself commented on the plethora of Sabbath practices in his day, making it quite clear that "the Sabbath was made for man, not man for the Sabbath" (Mark 2:27). One case of supposed Sabbath breaking was Yeshua's healing of a woman so bent over she could not straighten up at all (Luke 13:10–16). The Messiah's challenge of the accepted ruling from the oral law was intentional. If the *Mishnah* allowed for an ox or donkey to be untied from its stall on the Sabbath to be watered and fed, then why shouldn't a sick woman be released from her burden on the Sabbath day (verses 15–16)? The same can be said for many other traditions, such as the ruling that it was permissible for a son to vow to give funds to God instead of supporting his parents, perhaps by making a contribution to the temple treasury. But Yeshua made it quite plain that the fifth commandment ("Honor your father and your mother") was totally against any such arrangement for a Corban vow (Mark 7:9–11).

Obviously the Messiah did not intend that all tradition be thrown out, as he himself practiced many of the traditions in his earthly life and ministry. Many traditions smooth the way for a wholesome development of religious culture. Even the church has many traditions it follows as well.

THE MOSAIC LAW

Fruchtenbaum enters into a seven-argument discussion (pages 116–19) concerning whether the law of Moses can be the means by which to base Messianic Jewish practice. His arguments are sound in many respects, and his assessment is valid as far as the totality of the package of the Mosaic covenant is concerned. Yet we do need to take a closer look at this covenant.

The demise of this covenant was a painful one for the nation:

- No temple existed after A.D. 70.
- Therefore, no altar was present anymore.
- With no temple or altar present, the Levitical priests were unable to function in their ministry.

For these reasons, no wonder the religious leaders of the nation were in despair. The very heart of this covenant was no longer present, especially after the Council of Yavneh (A.D. 70–90) made Judaism a religion with no substitute atonement but now only repentance, prayer, and the godly lifestyle.

However, another look at the Mosaic covenant is necessary. The internal evidence of the book of Leviticus, which is an expansion of this covenant, demonstrates that four elements went into the Mosaic package (see page 90). Fruchtenbaum observes that elements of a previous covenant can be present in a succeeding covenant, but suggests that with the passing of the previous covenant and the establishment of a new one, the older one is no longer in force (page 122).

I will agree that because of the lack of a temple and an altar and the inability of Levitical priests to minister, the Mosaic covenant *as a total package* is no longer in force today. Even the Yavneh leaders recognized that a drastic change to the Mosaic covenant had occurred. But two of the elements from the Mosaic covenant are still present in the new covenant: the moral law of the Ten Commandments and the sacrificial system. Regarding the moral law, *Sha'ul* (Paul) himself referred to nine of the commandments in his letters as the means for proper behavior among the congregations; and while he did not mention the fourth commandment (about the Sabbath), he himself followed it as a *practice* in his life, even as an emissary among non-Jewish peoples (e.g., Acts 16:13). The moral law of the Ten Commandments continues as a part of the overall Word of God.

Fruchtenbaum opts to make a case for the commandments as a part of the law of Messiah because in his opinion the new covenant takes the place of the Mosaic covenant. But I would say that some of the Mosaic covenant is still in force because of the strong imprint of the moral code on the new covenant. Some believers view living out the love of God as led by the Spirit as the guideline for proper behavior under the Messiah; but genuine love has a moral base, which the commandments provide.

The element of the sacrificial system is also present, although all five sacrifices of the older covenant (sin, guilt, burnt, grain, and fellowship) are subsumed in the sacrifice of the Messiah.[8] I have noted in my response to William Varner (page 90) the connection between the Mosaic sin offering and the sin offering of the new covenant. The altar for the new covenant is the tree (execution-stake) on which Yeshua died (1 Peter 2:24), and the priesthood is the one to which the Messiah belongs, namely, that of Melchizedek (Hebrews 7:17). And so similarly, as with the element of the moral law of the Ten Commandments, something of the Mosaic covenant remains because of the strong tie between the element of the offerings of the Mosaic covenant and Yeshua's death.[9]

The element of the criminal and civil law codes is not transferred into the new covenant. When believers are convicted of crimes for which they will serve time in prison, they are not judged by local congregations; their cases are adjudicated by the courts of the states in which they live.

The last element deals with the model of worship (e.g., festivals) and lifestyle (e.g., dietary codes). If Gentile believers do

[8]As believers today, we relate to the sin offering once and for all, but we need to relate to the other four every day as we walk with the Lord, even as the Jewish writers affirm it in the New Covenant.

[9]One emphatic picture is the dedication offering of Leviticus 1, where the animal is consumed on the altar as a burnt offering. Yeshua became the example for us, likewise, to totally yield our lives as a burnt offering to the Lord, as *Sha'ul* (Paul) reminds us in Romans 12:1.

not wish to follow these models, they have the freedom to choose not to do so. Jewish believers are free from these practices if they choose to be members of a Gentile-culture church. On the other hand, members of Messianic congregations are free to participate in the various practices that make up a Jewish religious culture.

Across the centuries Jewish leaders have further developed these models and practices. Can this material appropriately be used? Our reply is a guarded yes, as long as a biblical theology guides the process to mark the acceptable choices. Sam Nadler has suggested that those who wish to be involved in Messianic congregations "accept the cultural distinctions, the language issues, the appreciation of Torah, the Messianic standards and garb that become the identity of the congregation, and so on. The Jewish believer does this, not because of legalism, but because of a calling based on a liberty which the New Covenant encourages."[10]

IDENTITY

Today many Christians declare they do not wish to take away the identity of the Jewish believer. Yes, he or she can affirm a heritage, study and speak Hebrew as the language in which to communicate, show solidarity with the Jewish community, remember the Holocaust, visit Israel, and so on. But as soon as the Jewish believer has a desire to participate in the Passover with his or her family, remember other holidays, wear the *kippah,* or cap, decline to eat pork or shellfish, worship on Saturday in a Messianic congregation, and so forth, he or she is told such practices put one "under the law," and therefore these activities cannot be a part of Christian doctrine and practice.

This has always been a puzzle for me. During the Great Awakening in the early 1700s, missionaries began their trek to the four corners of the earth to preach the Good News—and many people became believers. Medical doctors, nurses, and teachers soon followed, and hospitals, clinics, and schools were established in many countries where ministry was not only to the soul but to mind and body as well. In those early days,

---

[10]Sam Nadler, "What is Legalism? What is Liberty?"(unpublished paper).

people not only accepted the Lord, but they were also "civilized," that is, they took on a Western style of living. The result, as in Africa, was that believers' pagan cultures were set aside and they were given a belief system that was based on a Greek-culture context and lifestyle. It has only been since the middle of the last century that missionaries now realize that in sharing the Bible message it is acceptable to retain as much of a people's culture as possible, except when their pagan beliefs and practices are contrary to a biblical theology.

In the body of Messiah around the globe today, therefore, believers generally retain as much of their ethnicity and culture as possible so as to proclaim a message that can be most welcoming to unbelievers. But what about Jewish people? What can the Jewish believer do with his or her religious culture? While some non-Jewish believers realize that Jewish believers are entitled to their freedom to adhere to their customs, many still will say that the new Jewish believer must give up the practice of a culture that reflects the models of worship and lifestyle of the Mosaic covenant as well as that of the decisions of religious leaders over centuries, take on a non-Jewish lifestyle, and ease into the church's customs and practices.

Doesn't the Jewish believer have a freedom of choice as well? As long as we adhere to how Yeshua related to the practices, using what reflects a biblical point of view, and as long as we find the biblical base for an aspect of the oral law (which developed across the centuries), or adapt that particular aspect of the oral law, why can't we do the same as non-Jewish believers do in their cultures?

WORSHIP

The Messianic congregation makes use of the *siddur*[11] (or liturgy), which consists mostly of Scripture reading and prayers. The worship leader will combine his choices with suggestions

---

[11]Although many Messianic leaders have developed their own "home versions," two published *siddurim* widely used by Messianic congregations are: John Fischer and David Bronstein, *The Siddur for Messianic Jews* (Palm Harbor, Fla.: Menorah Ministries, 1988); and Jeremiah Greenberg, *The Messianic Shabbat Siddur* (Gaithersburg, Md.: Messianic Liturgical Resources, 1996).

that may come from the congregation at special times of consultation. The basic *Shabbat* (Sabbath) service, incorporated for Friday evening and Saturday morning services, is based on traditional observance but also includes Messianic adaptations and additions from Jewish prayer and praise passages in the gospels, letters, and Revelation.

Some prayers need to be carefully explained. For example, when a congregant has had a death in the family and asks the congregation to lead in the *kaddish* prayer, the leader should clearly state that this prayer gives glory to God and is designed to lift up the grieving person's spirit. In no way does the recitation of the prayer help the departed gain forgiveness of sins and an entrance into God's presence, as the traditional Jewish person hopes.

Already noted are the Passover as Yeshua adapted it (page 144) and the Day of Atonement from the Mosaic covenant and new covenant adaptation (page 144). In addition to holidays that relate to atonement, the Jewish calendar also includes freedom festivals, such as *Purim* (see the book of Esther), *Hanukkah*, or Dedication (see the book of 1 Maccabees), and *Yom HaShoah* (Holocaust Day). The acceptance by Messianic believers of those neutral cultural elements of Judaism not explicitly prohibited in Scripture is not an end in itself. We are reminded of our religious cultural heritage as Jewish people, but these occasions are also a means to present a biblical message, as our Messiah did in his earthly ministry. The Day of Atonement, in particular, can provide the opportunity to share with Jewish people the claims of Yeshua as the one who is our atonement for sin.

The practice of the ordinances[12] is also important. One of the ordinances of the congregation is immersion. Technically this is not to be regarded as the *mikveh* experience, which comes from the purification rite for women. The more acceptable word is *tebilah* (from *tabal*), with the basic idea of "to dip so as to cover" to describe immersion (Hebrew New Testament),[13] as it is used in Israel.

---

[12]Perhaps the closest word is *sav* (from *savah*), meaning "charge," or "command." *Sav* can mean "precept," and it would be a fitting word, but with no unanimity of opinion regarding these terms as yet, it is best continue to use "ordinance" for the time being.

[13]As, for example, Matthew 3:13–14 (Jerusalem: Keren Ahvah Meshihit, 2000).

The Hebrew word used in Israel for Messiah's communion is *se'udat haAdon* (1 Corinthians 11:20). The first word refers to the term *sa'ad*, meaning "to support," or "to refresh with a meal" (Judges 19:8; Psalm 104:15); this is the word used in the phrase for the third *Shabbat* meal—*se'udah shlishah*—taken late in the afternoon before the *Shabbat* ends.[14] Such a designation certainly captures the idea of the Lord's Table.

CONCLUSION

While some Jewish believers will exercise their freedom to find their fellowship in churches, others should have the opportunity to be involved in Messianic congregations, enjoying an identity that reaches back to the ancient patriarchs and will continue until the Messiah returns. As a result, children of Messianic Jewish believers will also have an exposure to Jewish culture and history that will give them an idea of who they are. And it is a testimony to the Jewish community at large that Messianic Jews do exist and believe in Yeshua and have not become non-Jews.

The body of Messiah here on earth consists of believers from many ethnic groups but all indeed are one in the Messiah. We cannot and must not rob any group of its cultural and ethnic contextualization. This applies to those of us who are Messianic Jews, as long as we maintain an authentic theology and an authentic Yeshua. Words are important in how we express our message, and no foreign lifestyle should be imposed that would take away the ethnic tie. Within the parameters of biblical principles, Jewish believers should have the freedom to worship Yeshua the Messiah in their own cultural framework. The body of Messiah will be richer for it.

---

[14]*The New Jewish Encyclopedia*, David Bridger and Samuel Wolk, eds. (New York: Behrman House, 1962), 416–17.

TORAH AND *HALAKHAH* AMONG MODERN ASSEMBLIES OF JEWISH YESHUA-BELIEVERS

An Israeli Response to Arnold Fruchtenbaum

Gershon Nerel

Keeping the Torah is commonly understood as part and parcel of maintaining Jewish identity. However, it is frequently disregarded that *only* the scriptural Torah—the canonical Pentateuch *(Torah Shebichtav* or *Torat Mosheh),* namely, the five books of Moses, alongside the sections of *Neviim* (Prophets) and *Ketuvim* (Writings) embodied in the Old Testament *(Tanakh)*—is accepted as a revelation from God. Within mainstream Judaism, the Oral Torah *(Torah Shebealpe),* also known as the *Halakhah,* is the rabbinical teachings and ceremonies accumulated throughout the ages that form the foundation for Jewish religious life. In light of this reality, too many modern Jewish believers in Yeshua (JBY) unfortunately also overestimate the *Halakhah* and fail to observe the scriptural Torah according to the teaching of the New Testament.

The *Halakhah,* consisting of rabbinical literature and depending on human traditions, actually stands apart from the sacred collection of the Bible. Furthermore, the *Halakhah* assumes an authority that was not given to it, aspiring to overmaster the authority of the Holy Bible. For example, the *Halakhah* unilaterally shifts the biblical New Year (Rosh Hashanah) from the month of Nisan, when Passover is kept at the springtime, to the fall. Consequently, an ongoing tension regarding authority exists between the scriptural Torah and the Oral Torah. This conflict over authority is further accelerated when discussing the New Testament, particularly the teachings of Yeshua.

Today, while bordering mainstream Judaism and functioning within a unique no-man's-land, JBY must provide clear answers to fundamental questions relating to Torah and the whole Bible on the one hand, and tradition and human authority on the other. In other words, which texts, in reality, are *the* exclusive basis for belief and practice? Which teachings and which customs are indeed obligatory and top priority, and which should be completely neglected? How does one outwardly express Jewish characteristics without compromising or even misleading the focus of Yeshua and the Bible? How does one establish a truthful but also practical system of priorities both for private and congregational life?

THE SUPREMACY OF THE WORDS OF YESHUA

As a matter of fact, only a handful of JBY do not accept the authority of the canonical Holy Scriptures comprising the Old and New Testaments as the Word of God. However, while JBY do not question the comprehensive validity of this canon, still too many among them, including Fruchtenbaum, do question the validity of the Mosaic covenant. Therefore, it should be underlined that in principle the writings of Moses are still valid for contemporary Jewish Yeshua-believers—yet they are fully subject to the teachings of Yeshua and the continuous guidance of the Holy Spirit.[1]

In order to relate rightly to the issue of the validity of the Torah, one should *not* start, as does Fruchtenbaum, with utilizing quotations from the epistles of the apostle Paul and commenting on them. Rather, one must refer initially to the words of Yeshua, the Son of God, as they appear in the Gospels. Putting the teachings of King Messiah in first place as the sole cornerstone for belief and practice, combined with the directives of the

[1]See, for example, my article, "Observing the Torah according to Yeshua," in *Chai*, the magazine of the British Messianic Jewish Alliance (Summer 2001), 1–5.

Spirit, enables one to discern which parts of the Torah are still relevant today and in what way they should relate to Jewish identity.

The very fact that Yeshua himself validated the Torah in a very authoritative way must be strongly emphasized. This is an elementary and cardinal matter. In his Sermon on the Mount Yeshua made this declaration:

> Do not think that I have come to abolish the Law [Torah] or the Prophets; I have not come to abolish them but to fulfill them. I tell you the truth, until heaven and earth disappear, not the smallest letter, not the least stroke of a pen, will by any means disappear from the law until everything is accomplished. Anyone who breaks one of the least of these commandments and teaches others to do the same will be called least in the kingdom of heaven, but whoever practices and teaches these commands will be called great in the kingdom of heaven.
>
> MATTHEW 5:17–19

Any exegetical attempts to minimize the significance of these words should be rejected. At the same time, however, nobody should take these words out of the entire context of the scattered words of Yeshua in the New Testament: that the only way of salvation is by faith in the crucified and resurrected Son of God—*not* by literally observing ceremonial practices of the Torah. And, for example, the baptism in water of new disciples of Yeshua is *not* in the name of the Torah but "in the name of the Father and of the Son and of the Holy Spirit, and teaching them to obey everything *I* have commanded you" (Matthew 28:19–20, emphasis added).

The Torah is still valid for JBY without the obsolete legalistic approaches of rabbis and sages who openly oppose the New Testament. Moreover, the specific rules and ordinances of the Torah relating to worship in the temple or to the Aaronic priesthood are no longer relevant today. It was Yeshua himself who foretold the destruction of the temple (Matthew 24:1–2), and he also explained that true worshipers of God do not need to go to Jerusalem (John 4:21–23). Obviously atonement and forgiveness of sins are no longer received through animal sacrifices and animal blood but only through the blood shed at Golgotha (Matthew 26:28; Mark 10:45; Luke 5:24). In the body of Messiah age in which we live, salvation comes only through belief in Yeshua (John 11:25–26).

In fact, the Torah did come to an end as a means of salvation, "for Messiah is the end of the law [Torah] *for righteousness*" (Romans 10:4 NASB, emphasis added). In addition, the Torah also ended as a guideline for punishment, either by "eye for eye, and tooth for tooth" (Matthew 5:38) or by stoning (John 8:3–11). But definitely the Torah of the Messiah did not cancel each and every aspect of the Pentateuch. The basic ethical principles of Torah are still valid for all humans. For example, who cancelled the Ten Commandments and other laws like social responsibilities for the poor and the widow (Leviticus 19:9–15), or who did away with the forbidding of acts of tattoo and sorcery (Leviticus 19:28, 31)? Similarly, Messiah Yeshua did not nullify the principle of respecting rulers and forbidding the cursing of leaders (Exodus 22:28). This principle was ratified also in the New Testament, when Saul/Paul faced the Jerusalem Sanhedrin and testified about his faith in Yeshua (Acts 23:5).

The Written Torah still has many aspects that are valid particularly for the people of Israel—in regard to the biblical calendar and feasts, for example. The Torah provides the elementary framework for keeping the Jewish nation—God's chosen people. As a distinct society, there must be a way for preserving the Jews uniquely in God's plan for history and beyond history.

When one realizes it was Yeshua himself who gave the Torah to Moses and to Israel on Mount Sinai, one can also easily see that in the New Testament Yeshua provides a new key as to how to keep the Torah in the new dispensation that started with the Incarnation. As the originator of the commandments in *both* Testaments, Yeshua has the full authority to introduce fresh guidelines and priorities regarding how to observe the Torah. Practically, therefore, while teaching in the New Testament to keep the Torah, Yeshua also modified it, not in any legalistic way, but by introducing instead new and higher insights for the kingdom of God.

THE INSTRUMENTALITY OF "MOSES' SEAT"

When it is both spiritually reasonable and practically possible, JBY should not totally ignore the rabbinical establishment. Even today, in a sense, the rabbinical leaders, the inheritors of the scribes and the Pharisees of antiquity, are still sitting "in Moses' seat" (Matthew 23:2). On that account, nowadays JBY may receive some "general services," so to speak, from rabbinical institutions.

Such services include, for example, wedding and burial functions. It should be noted that, according to the laws of the state of Israel, the approval of any Jewish beliefs and practices are left exclusively in the hands of the Orthodox religious leaders. This applies, for example, to the recognition of only those Jewish marriages that are conducted and approved by the official rabbinate. The same is true of the authorized last rites and burials for the Jewish society, even to the procurement of land for cemeteries and the decision of who will be buried there.

Thus, JBY couples may marry at the rabbinate offices, and even receive a *ketubah*, a marriage certificate, from them. Usually after such a rabbinical ceremony, congregations of JBY perform an additional matrimonial ceremony of their own, blessing the young couple in the name of Yeshua. But there are occasions when the Orthodox rabbis will reject JBY and refuse to do the wedding ceremony, and so these couples need to go outside the country, spending time and money abroad to get married. Most fly to Cyprus, the closest non-Arab country, for this occasion.

Another example is the service provided by *hevrah kadisha*, the burial societies. Actually, there is no reason why JBY should not employ the authorized Jewish burial societies and bury their dead in the formal Jewish cemeteries. In Israel, for example, some of the pioneer JBY, like Moshe Ben-Meir and Solomon Zeev Kofsman, were buried in the state cemeteries in Jerusalem. Yet, in other cases, the rabbis refused to supply a grave in the mainstream cemeteries. In such cases JBY had no choice but to bury their dead in alternate cemeteries—those belonging either to church organizations or to secular institutions.

In reality most of the rabbis and their delegates, either Orthodox, Conservative, or Reform, turn down these requests and deny any such services to JBY. Even though JBY are willing to follow certain procedures as mentioned above, still rabbinical Judaism often misuses its monopoly and manipulates its institutions against JBY through its long-lasting policy of "killing by delegitimization."

CIRCUMCISION

According to the commandment given to Abraham and his seed through Isaac forever ("This is my covenant with you and your descendants after you, the covenant you are to keep: Every male among you shall be circumcised" [Genesis 17:10]), God manifests his unique relationship with Israel. Yeshua, too, was circumcised on the eighth day (Luke 2:21). Nowadays circumcision on the eighth day remains both a religious and a national mark for the Jews, the eternal inheritors of the divine promises through Isaac and Jacob. The national and territorial promises to the Hebrews came hundreds of years prior to the presentation of the Torah to Moses on Mount Sinai. Presently these promises to Israel are still embodied symbolically in the act of circumcision.

At the same time, it must be absolutely clear that circumcision has nothing to do with gaining credit for salvation. Justification and salvation come only through faith in Yeshua and through his grace. This principle is equal for both Jew and non-Jew (Romans 4). Yet as a national symbol of the original covenant between God and Israel, circumcision remains a unique sign for the entire Jewish people, including JBY. Historically, the Judaizers of the first century wanted to impose circumcision also on the Gentiles, claiming that this operation was required for salvation (Acts 15:1). But that issue was long ago settled by the Jerusalem Council in the first century A.D. (Acts 15), namely, that circumcision in the flesh has nothing to do with salvation.

Another historical fact is that many churches continue, as in past generations, to request the abolition of circumcision by Jewish "converts," without really understanding the biblical background. Among us we still have elderly brethren who recall and testify that Gentile churches openly discredited them for circumcising their sons. Before the establishment of the state of Israel in 1948, it was not uncommon for JBY to face excommunication after circumcising their sons.[2]

As for the performance of the circumcision act, JBY in Israel find no difficulty at all in employing the services of professional and authorized circumcisers (*mohalim*) at the *Brit Mila* (circumcision) of their sons. Sometimes, however, when the parents of the baby tell the circumciser that they believe in Yeshua, the *mohel* will refuse to grant the full traditional blessing but will still perform the act for the sake of doing a good deed and getting a payment.

Nowadays the *Brit Mila* among JBY, both in Israel and the Diaspora, is actually a nonissue, since it is almost unanimously accepted as a national symbolic act, nowhere annulled *as such* in the New Testament.

THE SEVENTH-DAY SABBATH

The lunar calendar with its days of rest and feasts, as condensed in Leviticus 23, was nowhere in Scripture taken away and is therefore valid for JBY to observe. However, while keeping the biblical calendar with its special days, JBY should carefully discern between what *the* Rabbi says in the New Testament and what the establishment rabbis say. Only the guidelines of Yeshua should be considered by JBY for the observance of the seventh-day Sabbath, since "the Son of Man is Lord of the Sabbath" (Matthew 12:8).

In the state of Israel, for instance, the seventh-day Sabbath, rather than Sunday, is naturally observed by JBY as the day of rest and of worship. In some congregations the weekly service is held on Friday evening.[3] As a matter of fact, Yeshua also kept the Sabbath. But Yeshua always challenged the scribes and the Pharisees of his time and instructed them on how to observe the Sabbath. This correction should likewise apply to the current rabbinical establishment with its restrictions concerning the *Shabbat* observance. For example, because "the Sabbath was made for man, not man for the Sabbath" (Mark 2:27), it is fully

[2]See Gershon Nerel, "The Formation and Dissolution of a 'Messianic Jewish' (Hebrew Christian) Community in Jerusalem in the 1920s," in *Proceedings of the Twelfth World Congress of Jewish Studies*, Division E (Jerusalem 2001), 19–29 (Hebrew).

[3]See Kai Kjaer-Hansen and Bodil F. Skjott, *Facts and Myths about the Messianic Congregations in Israel*, Mishkan 30–31 (Jerusalem: Caspari Center, 1999), 221.

right for JBY to use a car and travel on the Sabbath to a Bible study or worship. Similarly, because "it is lawful to do good on the Sabbath" (Matthew 12:12), it is right for JBY to use fire and electricity for elementary activities. The same would apply for using money discreetly when circumstances require it.

At the same time, however, contemporary JBY should not stick to imposed *Shabbat* traditions, such as having candles on Friday evening and performing the ceremony of *Havdalah* (separation), applied to a special prayer declaring the end of the Sabbath. Benedictions over the *Shabbat* candles or over the *besamim*, the spices of the *Havdalah*, have no biblical foundation whatever, although rabbinical traditions introduced "divine" prayers and blessings as though they were ordained by God. Contrary to the *Halakhah* blessings during the lighting of candles, God did not command any JBY to perform these acts. Needless to say, traditional East-European food, like *gefilte* (stuffed) fish, has nothing to do with the observance of the Sabbath.

Likewise, JBY should *not* limit their *Shabbat* Bible study to the traditional weekly *parashah*, the Torah portions specified for public services in the synagogue. These divisions of the Torah, arranged in a one-year cycle, provide a preset and fixed text that anchors the study of the Bible within one bound framework. Any pattern of this kind sooner or later results in stagnancy and limits the guidance of the Spirit. Therefore such a restriction on the congregational teacher is not desirable. Moreover, while the study of Scripture in congregations of JBY does combine closely both covenants, and rightly so, still it should *not* start with the Old Testament. The starting point for each biblical study must rather begin with the New Testament perspective and focus on the "keys" provided by Yeshua.

The major issue of the seventh-day Sabbath is to rest from weekly obligations and to worship God. This holy day is to be used for the Lord and not for exhausting oneself through shopping, sports, or sightseeing at the expense of taking quality time for spiritual growth and edification.

PASSOVER

Since biblical *Pesach* (Passover) is not linked to the Gregorian church calendar, JBY do not need to correlate this feast to the church's Easter, but they should celebrate it together with the rest of the Jewish people. This is *the* major Messianic feast, emphatically pointing from the Old Testament to the characteristics pertaining to the Messiah: the sacrificial lamb and the atoning blood. This is the feast whereby Jewish people especially can understand the meaning of "the Lamb of God, who takes away the sin of the world!" (John 1:29).

The center of the *Pesach* celebration should not be the reading of the traditional *Haggadah,* the narrative of the exodus from Egypt. Indeed, the remembrance of Israel's redemption from Egypt is significant, but it is even more important to remember the redemption through Yeshua from the bondage of sin. The *Pesach* should primarily be a reminder of the Last Supper of Yeshua and his command to commemorate his death and resurrection. Because the Passover meal is especially meant for the younger generation—to educate the children—time management is of utmost importance so as to not waste time on insignificant matters. Thus the *Pesach* ceremony must not relate to marginal issues considered important by tradition, such as reading lengthy portions from the Talmud or singing Aramaic songs like *Had Gadya* (meaning "An Only Kid"), hardly understood by children.

In other words, as JBY celebrate *Pesach,* it is sufficient to use only the relevant texts from Scripture. For example, such texts are clearly found in Exodus 12, where the connection is quite clear between the blood of each Passover lamb on each Jewish home and the death of the Messiah. Here, with the blood of the lamb on the lintel and the two doorposts of each house, one can also observe the symbol of the cross. Another text may relate to the fulfillment of Isaiah 53. Eventually the whole celebration should be connected with the Lord's Supper, reminding the people of Yeshua's victory over sin.[4]

In addition, during *Pesach* JBY should eat only the *mazza,* the unleavened bread, symbolizing abstaining from sin and the challenge to live a holy life.[5] The feast of *mazzot* reminds us of

[4]See Benjamin and Ruben Berger, *Bereitet dem Herrn den Weg!* (Hombrechtikon: Echad, 1993), 53–63. Cf. Gershon Nerel, *Messianic Jews in Eretz-Israel (1917–1967)* (Dissertation, Hebrew University, Jerusalem 1996), 227.

[5]See Michal Charish, "Not on the Mazza Alone," in *Kivun* (Jerusalem), vol. 27 (2002), 8–9 (Hebrew).

the importance of "the unleavened bread of sincerity and truth" (1 Corinthians 5:8, NASB). Most Israeli JBY eat only *mazza* during the *Pesach* week. The same kind of bread is used during the rest of the year for the other occasions of celebrating Communion.

KASHRUT (KOSHER FOOD)

Whereas the Old Testament dietary laws were primarily given for the Jews, the New Testament also instructs Gentile believers to distinguish between food that is *kasher* (permissible) and *terefah* (forbidden). The council of apostles at Jerusalem decided even the Gentile believers should "abstain from things sacrificed to idols, from blood, from the meat of strangled animals" (Acts 15:29). Basically and wherever possible, JBY should keep the dietary laws of *kashrut*, avoiding meat such as pork, seafood, and creeping animals. In the state of Israel it is no problem for JBY to keep the elementary dietary laws of *kashrut*, although obviously such abstaining has nothing to do with salvation or achieving a higher spiritual status.[6]

The apostle *Sha'ul* (Paul) also makes it very clear that one should not be legalistic in these matters. As in the case of observing *Shabbat*, both logic and the guidance of the Spirit must be used in order to eat and bless the food, with thanksgiving (1 Timothy 4:1–5). Moreover, as with disciples of Yeshua from all the nations, JBY should likewise *not* make the issue of food a source of arguments and quarreling. The proper principle has to be as follows: "Eat anything sold in the meat market without raising questions of conscience" (1 Corinthians 10:25).

This principle applies not only to buying in shops but also when being invited as guests to a meal, when totally unable to control the circumstances. In such cases much sensitivity and flexibility need to be practiced. Often also much creativity is needed, and nowadays even in the Diaspora it is common to ask for a vegetarian meal. It is not difficult at all to ask for "health food" and so to keep the *kashrut*.

Practically, JBY accept the rabbinical rules of ritual slaughtering and need not develop their own system of supervising the

---

[6]See Moshe Emmanuel Ben Meir, *From Jerusalem to Jerusalem—Excerpts from Diary* (Jerusalem 2001), 88 (Hebrew).

slaughtering of animals and the distribution of meat. JBY should also remind themselves of the principle that it *is* permissible for Jews to mix milk and meat. The Torah only forbids the slaughtering of the young-born animal together with the mother: "Do not cook a young goat in its mother's milk" (Exodus 23:19; 34:26).

HANUKKAH AND CHRISTMAS

Hanukkah (Feast of Dedication) is explained in the apocryphal book of Maccabees as a commemoration of the victory of the Jews over the Syrians in 165 B.C. The festival is mentioned once in the New Testament (John 10:22), yet there is no commandment whatsoever to observe this feast. We may compare this situation with the text mentioning the first disciples who sold their private property and shared everything in a communal life (Acts 4:32–37) in that there is no biblical commandment that all believers must always live in a communal system without private belongings.

The celebration of Hanukkah by lighting candles for eight days—as a reminder of the miracle of the cruse of oil that burned for eight days instead of one—introduces a "divine benediction" on the candles that was never given by God. God never commanded the lighting of such candles. This is a traditional festival and should not be imposed on JBY. In the state of Israel, for example, children do celebrate Hanukkah with their peers in the kindergarten and in the schools, but this festival has no meaning for congregational life, particularly as it has no Messianic significance rooted in the Bible.

According to *Halakhah,* Hanukkah begins on the 25th day of the Jewish month of Kislev, and it stands as a counterpart for Christmas, Feast of the Messiah. Within the Jewish commonwealth one can easily observe how the Hanukkah celebrations appear to be interchangeable with Christmas. In order to avoid confusions between these two feasts of light, JBY should celebrate the Festival of the Messiah, and not Hanukkah, to highlight the significance of the Incarnation and the fulfillment of the numerous Messianic prophecies in the Bible. The specific dates of December 24/25 are not important, but only the fact that, as an act of solidarity with all believers in the Messiah in the world,

JBY share in the greatest event in history. In this way JBY keep the spiritual proportions with regard to celebrating the festivals. The festival of Yeshua's advent into this world is more significant than the Festival of Dedication, even though this festival is not ordained in Scripture.

PURIM

Like Hanukkah, Purim represents the victory of the Jews over their enemies. Interestingly, however, while the book of Esther is included in the scriptural canon, the name of God does not appear in the book. In reality, the Feast of Purim has become a carnival of costumes and of silly activities. During this feast it is permissible for minors to smoke cigarettes, and the celebrants are encouraged to get drunk. According to *Halakhah,* it is a "Mitzvah" (religious duty) to dine and drink.

Unlike Hanukkah, Purim is not mentioned in the New Testament. From a national viewpoint, in the state of Israel, for example, children annually celebrate this feast and remember the deliverance of the Jews from their foes. Yet Purim should not have a role in the congregational life of JBY. There is no biblical or theological justification to celebrate this feast, as it has no linkage whatsoever to the Messiah. The national identity of JBY is not weakened when they do not celebrate Purim in their assemblies. In fact, during the second temple period Purim did not possess a canonized status among the festivals of Israel.[7]

Neither Purim nor Hanukkah brought lasting victory—or comprehensive salvation—for the Jewish people. The enemies and haters of Israel have not disappeared. Modern "Hamans" and "Antiochuses" are still fighting against the Jews. The only comfort and hope for Israel is in Yeshua.

NO NEED FOR A MESSIANIC *HALAKHAH*

Because JBY are totally free of keeping the *Torah shebaal peh,* the oral law, they should not develop their own *Halakhah* based

[7]See, for example, Aharon Oppenheimer, "'Love of Mordechai or Hatred of Haman'? Purim in the Days of the Second Temple and Afterwards," in *Zion* 62 (Jerusalem 1997): 408–18 (Hebrew).

on those customs and decrees originating from non-believers in Yeshua. In fact, the modern followers of the so-called *hazal*, the Jewish sages, still reject Yeshua and oppose his teachings. How can the deniers of Yeshua set an example for JBY?

There are explicit cases where the New Testament and *Halakhah* sharply clash. First, when praying, men among JBY should not wear a cap *(kippah)* on their heads, against the practice of some JBY today. In the New Testament we read that during worship men should take off their hats (1 Corinthians 11:7). Second, it is no secret that within mainstream synagogues JBY are unwelcome as persona non grata. Since the name of Yeshua is still anathema in the normative synagogues, why do JBY need to use the term *beit-knesset* (synagogue) for their assemblies? *Kehila* (congregation) is a preferable term, since it does not hold any connotations to the *minim* (meaning "apostates" and referring to JBY) mentioned in the regular *siddur*, the Jewish prayer book.

The only teacher of JBY must be Yeshua, not the *hazal*. It is the duty and responsibility of JBY to focus totally on the teachings of Yeshua and the guidance of the Holy Spirit. Therefore, JBY should remind themselves of the words of Yeshua concerning the rabbis and their traditions: "Hypocrites! You shut the kingdom of heaven in men's faces" (Matthew 23:13)—and especially these words: "Woe to you experts in the law [Torah], because you have taken away the key to the knowledge. You yourselves have not entered, and you have hindered those who were entering" (Luke 11:52).

CONCLUSION

Because Torah does not only mean "law" and "ordinances" (Greek, *nomos*), but also "teaching" and "educating" (Greek, *didachē*), it is of utmost significance for modern JBY to carefully observe the Torah of the Messiah, first given in the Old Testament and later revised in the New Testament. All the teachings and ordinances of Yeshua, as the ultimate and divine authority, should be understood and implemented by JBY through the guidance of the Holy Spirit.

It is absolutely true that Yeshua broke down the dividing wall of hostility between Jewish believers and other believers in Yeshua from the nations (Ephesians 2:11–16). Yet at the same time, Yeshua did *not* establish another wall between JBY and the Torah. Just as there is a spiritual unity around the Messiah between Jews and Gentiles, in a real sense JBY still have a physical and ethnic unity with the whole nation of Israel.

It should be emphasized that the fence Yeshua removed is not the Written Torah or the national commandments. The fence Yeshua removed, with the destruction of the second temple, was the Mosaic covenant. While all five of the Levitical offerings are now a part of the one sacrifice of the Messiah, his sacrifice now provides a focus on salvation for all peoples, Jews and Gentiles alike, who become a part of the one body of the Messiah. And so Saul/Paul wrote, "Carry each other's burdens, and in this way you will fulfill the law [Torah] of Messiah" (Galatians 6:2).

IN SEARCH OF . . . A JEWISH IDENTITY

A Response to Arnold Fruchtenbaum

William Varner

Arnold Fruchtenbaum has played a very important role during the development of the Messianic movement over the last twenty-five years. He directs a ministry that encourages both the growth of individual Jewish believers and the growth of Messianic congregations. His writings have contributed greatly to the movement, and this writer has benefited often from them. He has especially helped to provide a theological foundation for "Hebrew Christianity."[1]

As I ponder Fruchtenbaum's chapter, I am struck negatively not so much by what he has written but by what he has *not* written. While I expected his chapter to be primarily an apologetic for the existence of Messianic congregations, it does not take that direction at all. He actually spends most of the chapter critically evaluating, in his words (page 112), "many Messianic congregations whose doctrinal position I question and whose worship style allows all kinds of 'wild things' to occur—and there is nothing Jewish about them." As a matter

[1]See especially his *Hebrew Christianity: Its Theology, History, and Philosophy* (Grand Rapids: Baker, 1974), and *Israelology: The Missing Link in Systematic Theology* (Tustin, Calif.: Ariel Ministries Press, 1993).

of fact, he very effectively points out the numerous biblical/theological problems with much of the movement, especially the more "Torah Observant" wing.

His criticisms of (1) their wrong emphasis on the role of the Mosaic law, (2) their overemphasis on rabbinic Judaism, and (3) their wrong stress on the importance of Jewish ritual observance all are effectively and very convincingly presented. I agree with his critical comments about these problematic areas. Therefore, at that level, I can find very little to critically evaluate in his chapter. He has effectively pointed out both the real and potential problems that characterize much of the movement.

THE MISSING QUESTION

As I mentioned, my concern about his chapter is not so much in what he wrote as in what he did not write. Let me put it simply. If Messianic congregations are an acceptable practice to follow in the practical ministry of the gospel (and that is still the question that needs to be demonstrated), then the way Fruchtenbaum describes them is the way they should be maintained. It appears that he constantly makes every unique characteristic of Messianic congregations totally optional and not something to be required by their leaders. He constantly stresses the principle of freedom on the part of the individual Jewish believer to participate or not to participate in the more Jewish observances in these congregations.

All this is well and good (in my opinion), but it all still begs the question about whether or not there should even be a movement of Messianic congregations, especially outside the land of Israel. It is this grand assumption he makes for the validity of these congregations that I would still like to see defended and not just assumed. Early in his chapter (pages 111–12), Fruchtenbaum asks and answers three basic questions:

1. If the question is asked, "Are Messianic congregations a biblical necessity or requirement?" then the answer has to be no.
2. If the question is asked differently, "Is it biblically permissible to have Messianic Jewish congregations?" then the answer is yes.

3. If yet a third question is asked, "Is it mandatory for Jewish believers to attend only Messianic Jewish congregations?" again the answer is no.

My response is that these are not the only questions that should be asked and answered. Perhaps a fourth one should be, "*Should* there even be Messianic congregations?" (not just "Are they permissible?"). This question is simply not addressed, and Fruchtenbaum proceeds to develop his chapter assuming that the answer is yes to this unmentioned fourth question.

I kept looking for Fruchtenbaum to develop a biblical apologetic for Messianic congregations, but I did not find what I was expecting. What I did read was a very effective critique of abuses in the movement, but not a defense of the very existence of the movement as scripturally legitimate. It is this assumption—some may even call his "begging of the question"—that is the weakest part of the chapter for the reader who still has questions about the legitimacy of "Messianic Judaism."

THE CULTURAL ISSUE

Fruchtenbaum's only real effort to justify the existence of these congregations seems to be the "cultural" reason given as an answer to his proposed second question (page 112): "Jewish believers have the right to set up uniquely ethnic Jewish congregations that reflect the Jewish culture and style of music, worship, teaching, and so on, just as Black, Latino, and Chinese churches would reflect their particular style of worship and culture." Fruchtenbaum sees this as a "neutral issue."

The contextualizing of theology has been a major issue, especially in missiology, over the past few decades.[2] The question of the degree to which timeless truths are to be communicated in certain cultures has engaged scholars in the fields of intercultural studies, linguistics, and biblical theology. This is certainly not the place to offer even a preliminary evaluation of

---

[2]Many trace this to the work of Donald McGavran, Charles Kraft, and their colleagues at Fuller Theological Seminary's School of World Mission. Fuller professor Arthur Glasser has especially stressed the role of contextualization in relation to Jewish evangelism in a number of published and unpublished writings.

such a complex and important issue facing everyone who wishes to communicate the gospel in a scripturally faithful and culturally sensitive manner. These issues will continue to be on the missiological agenda for years to come.

My immediate concern is Fruchtenbaum's perspective that this issue of Jewish congregations is no different from Latino and Chinese churches reflecting their particular worship and culture. Is this really a fair comparison?

Many ethnic churches in America justify their existence because either (1) the congregants come from another country, or (2) the congregants' first language is not English. In a strange land with a strange language all around them, members of ethnic churches find encouragement and comfort where the Word of God is spoken in their first language and where their unique problems as "strangers" are faced along with others who are also encountering those same problems. Can this really be applied to the situation facing Jewish people in America? American Jews are not immigrants speaking another language (apart from a small group of Russian immigrants), and they are not usually as culturally distinct from other Americans as are Chinese and Latinos. Is the American Jewish culture such that we should argue for Yiddish-speaking congregations? I am sure that Fruchtenbaum would not insist on this, except in extremely rare circumstances. I only point this out to show the weakness of this "cultural" argument to justify Messianic congregations.

I am very aware that America is not the only country where Jewish people live. In my chapter I suggested that there may be a stronger reason to justify Messianic congregations in Israel (for example, where the language is Hebrew and the culture is a religious Jewish one). In Israel Jewish holidays and customs are more a part of the national culture, unlike the situation in other countries. Fruchtenbaum's model would be more appropriate in such a context.

MORE QUESTIONS

I offer a few further observations and questions about issues that were not addressed in Fruchtenbaum's chapter.

What implications do the developments in Jewish life from A.D. 70 to 135 have for justifying Messianic congregations?

Can we simply return to the conditions in Judea prior to the destruction of the temple in A.D. 70 for our model of congregational life?

Do not the decisions at Yavneh in the decades following A.D. 70 make re-creating the situation in the early church impossible?

Does not the "parting of the ways" between church and synagogue make many of the arguments for Messianic congregations a bit anachronistic?

Does not the refusal to address these questions indicate a historical myopia on the part of those who want to re-create conditions that cannot be re-created in light of historical events and decisions by the rabbis since the book of Acts?

Another historical question that concerns me was one I mentioned in my own chapter. What steps are being taken to prevent a repeat of the historical degeneration of the orthodox first-century Nazarenes into the decidedly unorthodox second- and third-century Ebionites? Was not a characteristic of Ebionism that it emphasized Jewish observances in a similar way to what we see today in many sections of Messianic Judaism? Should we also be concerned about attempts on the part of some to redefine very basic doctrinal verities like the Trinity and the deity of Jesus? Are such attempts at contextualization in Jewish terms surrendering more than is necessary?

On the other end of the historical spectrum lies another question. Why is it that this question about Messianic congregations is being asked at this specific time? Why is it that, apart from a very small movement in Eastern Europe at the turn of the nineteenth century, Jewish believers never significantly argued for distinctly Messianic synagogues until recently? Why is it that the movement appeared in a significant way only in the last twenty-five years? What has occurred to cause this change?

What happened to the idea of "Hebrew Christian fellowships" within a Bible-believing church? This practice was followed faithfully by many Jewish believers for generations. Why has it been abandoned by many in favor of separate congregations? Why have some former firm advocates of the Hebrew Christian fellowship alternative (including Fruchtenbaum!) now switched to advocating the establishment of separate Jewish congregations?

I would be happy to see attempted answers to these questions as part of an apologetic for Messianic congregations. I did not find these questions addressed by Dr. Fruchtenbaum in his chapter.

THE IDENTITY ISSUE

The last issue I wish to raise concerns the only real purpose that Fruchtenbaum sees for having a Messianic congregation. He demonstrates clearly that it is simply not a good argument that Messianic congregations are the best way to reach out to unbelieving Jewish people because most Jewish members of Messianic congregations did not come to the Messiah through the witness of a Messianic congregation (page 115). He then concludes that the primary purpose for Messianic congregations is not for the sake of the unbelieving Jewish community but for the sake of the believing Jewish community—for the establishing of a Messianic Jewish culture (page 115).

Fruchtenbaum concludes (page 116) that the purpose of this section of his chapter is "to defend biblically the [Messianic community's] right to its Jewish identity." The problem is that no arguments are offered to defend this "right." It is only assumed that this is a noble and worthy and scriptural motive. The rest of his chapter actually is a criticism of those Messianic Jews who wrongly emphasize the law in seeking to maintain their "Jewish identity." Again, my criticism is not in what he wrote but in what he did not write. Is the assumption that Jewish believers *ought* to seek to maintain their "Jewish identity" a valid one in light of Scripture's teaching about a believer's new identity?

I offer a few concluding thoughts on this issue of whether or not it is important for Jewish believers to make a concerted effort to establish Jewish congregations to maintain their "Jewish identity." Has this matter of Jewish identity been overemphasized? Are there biblical teachings that are being ignored in such efforts? Some will find it easy to dismiss these words because of my Gentile background. I only ask that readers try to consider this issue biblically, not personally. Believe me when I say that my sympathy for the problems of Jewish believers is far greater than can be expressed in words. Believe me also when I say that true identity for the believer is not to be sought in culture but in a Person.

Identity for the Jewish Believer

Everyone engaged in sharing the Good News with Jewish people knows that a strong sense of Jewish identity can be a stumbling block to an unsaved Jewish person who considers faith in Jesus. It often is overlooked, however, that a strong sense of Jewish identity may also be a stumbling block to a Jewish believer's sanctification in Jesus.[3] If the focus of Messianic congregations is on establishing, preserving, or maintaining the members' "Jewish identity," then a major obstacle to real and vital spiritual growth may be created. Is there an alternative to "Jewish identity" in light of the New Testament evidence? Consider what the New Testament teaches about a believer's identity: A believer's identity should be shaped (1) by the terminology of the Bible and (2) by his spiritual position as a believer.

The apostle Paul, possibly the most famous Jewish believer of all time, tells us that his identity was not found in his Jewish culture but in Christ (Philippians 3:4–9). His desire was "to be found in him" (verse 9), not to find his identity in his culture or even in his people. Some Jewish believers vehemently reject the term "Christian" because of its association with Catholicism and with Jewish persecution through the years. I would not argue that "Christian" carries no cultural baggage, but I am reminded that one of the three times the term is used in the New Testament the Jewish believer Peter uses it as a positive term: "However, if you suffer as a Christian, do not be ashamed, but praise God that you bear that name" (1 Peter 4:16). Granted, "Christian" is not the only term in the New Testament for a follower of Christ. The terms "brother" and "saint" are used far more often. Also, the word "believer" is prominent (see, for example, Acts 2:44; 10:45; 16:1). Many, therefore, prefer the term "Jewish believer" to clarify their background and their new faith. But the term "Messianic Jew" is nowhere used in the New Testament and also carries its own confusion in that any Jewish person believing in a future Messiah could be called a "Messianic Jew." Far more serious is that the term "Jew" sometimes becomes the

---

[3]I want to thank Bruce Scott for his helpful insights in his unpublished paper, "Christ Is All: Discovering a Biblical Identity for Jewish Believers" (November, 2000).

operative word in the title and not the word "Messianic." Is not this a subtle but dangerous shift of emphasis with regard to one's identity?

But arguments about words and titles are not the main problem in the issue of Jewish identity. Far more important is the New Testament teaching about where and how a Jewish believer's identity is found. Texts like 2 Corinthians 5:17 and Galatians 3:28 are key in this regard. To Paul, every believer is a "new creation"—something that didn't exist before. That new person was not to be defined by fleshly distinctions—be those distinctions male or female, slave or free, or even Jew or Gentile! While these distinctions still exist, of course, they are not where one's identity is now to be found! The core truth, therefore, for a new believer, whatever his or her background, is this: "Christ is all, and is in all" (Colossians 3:11).

Christ is the end of the law for righteousness (Romans 10:4), and Christ also is the end of the search for identity ("For to me, to live is Christ" [Philippians 1:21]). Adding anything to the believer's biblical identity results in questioning the very sufficiency of Christ himself. Accentuating one's Jewishness, in light of the above texts, may in the long run lead to retarded spiritual growth at the best, or to pride and self-sufficiency at the worst. Since "from now on we recognize no one according to the flesh" (2 Corinthians 5:16 NASB), the best solution to the issue of Jewish identity is the believer's own spiritual position in Christ.

These words should not be interpreted to mean that I think Dr. Fruchtenbaum is guilty of retarding his own or others' growth by his position. I hope that he would agree with the general thrust of what I have written. I only offer these words as a warning to those espousing Messianic congregations as a means of maintaining their Jewish identity. Is maintaining one's ethnic identity really what any believer should be vitally concerned about—whether he is Chinese, Latino, African-American, or Jewish? Whatever his background, from the moment of regeneration, a believer in Jesus Christ (or, if you prefer, Yeshua haMashiach) should no longer define himself according to worldly, fleshly standards and distinctions. Even though he may still retain these outward distinctions, they should not matter to him anymore. All that should matter now is who he is in Christ.

I would like to thank Arnold Fruchtenbaum for his overall contribution to the Messianic movement and also for his specific warnings about the excesses of Messianic Judaism in his chapter. I would simply ask that he and others in the movement address some of these issues I have raised. What is still needed in my opinion is a scriptural apologetic for Messianic congregations that is sensitive to historical and theological issues as well as to the limitations of contextualization.

SUMMARY ESSAY: THE FUTURE OF MESSIANIC JUDAISM

David H. Stern[1]

I am known in the Messianic Jewish movement for five books I have written (see the preface, page 10). But since 1998, when people have asked me, "What book are you working on now?" I have answered, "None. I'm working on personal issues." This is because until then I had been so much of a "head person" that I had put matters of the heart aside. I was thus unaware of my deep inner needs and unaware of my pain in not having them met. I tolerated in myself sin that should have been confessed and not allowed to continue. In the past five years God has given me much healing, so that I have been able to turn from that sin. In the process I have come to see how important it is for all of us to get emotional and spiritual healing for our own individual sakes, for the sake of the movement, and for the sake of the Messiah's body. I mention this here, at the start of the article, because this autobiographical fact has heavily influenced what I have written.

SUCCESS STORY?

Writing about the future of Messianic Judaism is a daunting challenge. To meet it, I am combining the roles of forecaster,

[1]David H. Stern is using his own translation—the *Complete Jewish Bible*—for all biblical quotations.

futurist, and prophet. Forecasters base their predictions on available relevant data, so here are some facts and figures: In 1988 I wrote in *Messianic Jewish Manifesto* that there were in the United States 50,000 to 100,000 Jewish believers in Yeshua and over 120 Messianic Jewish congregations. Today America must have more like 200,000 Jewish believers and at least 300 Messianic Jewish congregations. I wrote that in Israel there might be 1,000 to 3,000 Jewish believers in 25 to 30 congregations, whereas now there are between 2,500 and 10,000 Jewish believers in some 90 congregations.[2] In 1988 there were the bare beginnings of a couple of Messianic Jewish educational institutions in the U.S. and none in Israel; today there are at least three flourishing Messianic Jewish seminaries, or *yeshivas,* in the U.S. and two in Israel. Moreover, the movement has spread geographically. Since the Iron Curtain fell, more than one hundred Messianic Jewish congregations, as well as schools, have been developed in the former Soviet Union and Eastern Europe. One of these, in Kiev, is probably the largest Messianic Jewish congregation in the world, with over a thousand members. The movement has also begun to take hold in Latin America, with congregations and schools from Mexico to Brazil and Argentina. Not bad growth over the course of a decade and a half!

Data evidencing the Jewish aspects of the Messianic Jewish congregations are harder to come by. I would guess that 10 to 20 percent of them have Torah scrolls. A much larger percentage celebrate the major Jewish holidays in some fashion. A significant number of their members light *Shabbat* candles. Observance of *kashrut* (the dietary laws) varies from not at all to the fairly careful separating of meat and milk (a rabbinic ordinance).

I could try to find more statistics documenting our institutions and other physical aspects of our success as a movement. But it would be a mistake—first, because our movement's "success," if such a word is even appropriate, should be measured by spiritual and not physical criteria; and second, because in my opinion we have a history of triumphalism, by which I mean

---

[2]David H. Stern, *Messianic Jewish Manifesto* (Clarksville, Md.: Jewish New Testament Publications, 1988), 197–98. See also Kai Kjaer-Hansen, *Myths and Facts about the Messianic Congregations in Israel* (Jerusalem: Caspari Center, 1998–99).

declaring victory before it has happened. It's too easy to become unduly proud of our achievements, and this can quickly get in the way of further achievement! A personal experience will explain what I mean.

When I was nineteen, I led a group of Boy Scouts on a summer outing in Yosemite National Park. One day we decided to climb Mount Dana, the park's second-highest peak. We started at Tioga Pass, 10,000 feet above sea level, and the summit is 13,000 feet above sea level. It's not a complicated climb—just keep putting one foot in front of the other and follow the trail to the top. The fourteen- and fifteen-year-olds took off like a shot, and I didn't see them for the next five hours. But eleven-year-old Don Page was a fat, unathletic kid, like I was at his age. Within minutes he was huffing and puffing, and his pace had slowed. As the responsible adult, I decided I should stick with him. After walking through the scrawny pines for a few hundred yards, he asked an astonishing question: "Are we on top yet?" After a moment's thought I simply said, "No, not yet; let's keep going." But ten minutes later he asked again, "Are we on top yet?" This time I explained, "No, the top is where you can look down in every direction. As you see, the trail continues uphill. Keep climbing, don't give up!" Fifteen minutes later: "Is this the top?" "No, Don, but you'll get there. You can do it!" And so on, every few minutes, the same question. But finally, at 1:30 in the afternoon, forty-five minutes after the next-slowest hiker, we arrived at the summit. And, boy, was he happy! He had truly accomplished what he had set out to do.

But if in answer to any one of his questions I had said, "Yes, Don, this is the top," he would have been just as happy. And he would have felt the same pride of accomplishment. The only trouble is that my answer wouldn't have been true. So his pride would have been false and unjustified, even though he wouldn't have known it.

I don't want us Messianic Jews to think we have arrived when we haven't. Achievements in our movement are real, yet they are not a reason to settle into our comfort zone. We have accomplished much, yet we must brace for continuous and lengthy effort in order to reach our goals. Nevertheless, like Don, we'll get there. We can do it!—because God is with us and gives us strength (see Isaiah 8:10; Philippians 4:13).

CRISIS AND GOALS

It may seem that we need only remind ourselves of what our goals are and then set out to reach them. This is the world's way, but it can't be ours. The faith we have implies doing everything in the presence of God. Both choosing our goals and reaching them must be done in an intimate relationship with him. And in this regard the American Messianic Jewish movement at present faces a crisis—a crisis of faith. This crisis has a generational aspect common to many movements: The children of the founders have to find their own way of leading. Like Yochanan (John) I want to speak directly to both the parents and the children (1 Yochanan [1 John] 2:12–14).

> You parents, you who came to faith in the exciting period of the Jesus Movement in the late 1960s and 1970s, your love and ardor for Yeshua, together with your excitement at the idea that you could believe in him and still stay Jewish, worked to make you a generation of zealous, enthusiastic leaders. With the rest of the Boomer Generation you were tired of materialism and sought a more spiritual path, and you found the right answer to your quest in Yeshua. With your pioneering spirit you created the Messianic Jewish movement as it is now. But many of you have allowed yourselves to become entangled in its institutionalism and bureaucracy, refining its theology and practices and generating finances. In the process you have left your first love. You have retreated into your heads, and your hearts are dying. Like Yochanan in the book of Revelation, I call you to return to your first love—Yeshua the Messiah of Jews and Gentiles alike. Without him, your great talents will dry up the movement. "Therefore, remember where you were before you fell, and turn from this sin, and do what you used to do before" (Revelation 2:4–5).
>
> But you children—the children of these leaders—you were born into believing families and don't remember having had the experience of coming from unbelief to faith. I see you as struggling to find out who you are and what will give purpose and meaning to your life. Your contemporaries, Generation X, are a lost generation, the Ernest Hemingways and F. Scott Fitzgeralds of our

time. A few years ago the Union of Messianic Jewish Congregations conference called you the "Joshua Generation"—ready, like him, to receive the scepter of authority in the movement from your aging "Moses" parents. But the conferees failed to see that, except for Joshua and Caleb, that entire generation died in the wilderness! Don't die! There's life in Yeshua—eternal life—and he will give new life to you and to the Messianic Jewish movement if you will only seize the opportunity and not settle for the easy existence you could readily choose. Find the challenges and meet them! If you are lukewarm, Yeshua will spew you out of his mouth (Revelation 3:15–22)!

So there is an urgency to my message. The American Messianic Jewish movement can either settle back, becoming just another religious denomination, or it can spring ahead, discerning what Yeshua's goals for the movement are and looking to him for the wisdom and energy to reach them. (The situation in Israel for Messianic Jews is different, because here the movement is still in its pioneering phase; I will have more to say about it later.)

However, one purpose is central to every goal we or any group of believers might have, and it is to live in the presence of God—our Father in heaven, his Son who died for us and rose again, and the Holy Spirit filling us always. Without abiding in God, we can be a political movement, a therapy group, or a social club, but not the body of Messiah.

To forward the expression of our faith in a Messianic Jewish way, I propose six goals, all subsidiary to this one purpose. There are others, some of them mentioned briefly in the final section of this essay and arguably more important than those noted here, but these are the ones I want us to look at now:

- seeking emotional healing
- defining and pursuing community
- developing a proper expression of Jewishness
- engaging in evangelism
- preparing for the land of Israel to become the center of Messianic Judaism
- refining our theology so as to help end the schism between the body of Messiah and the Jewish people

Seeking Emotional Healing

We can achieve these goals. Yes, we can do it! But the *doing* our movement requires is not our first priority. Our first priority is *being*, not doing; and this *being* is primarily an individual experience, not a communal one. Developing Messianic Judaism is a communal task, but before we can function effectively as a community most of us need emotional healing as individuals. Thus the *being* that we need is individually being in the presence of God and receiving his love, so that we can give love to God and to others. Love is our first and final spiritual criterion. Yeshua said that the two most important *mitzvot* were to love God and to love other people (Mark 12:28–31; cf. Leviticus 19:18; Deuteronomy 6:5); moreover, his "new commandment" to us as his disciples was to love one another as he himself loves us (Yochanan [John] 13:34–35). The Bible's "love chapter" teaches that anything we do that is not motivated by love has no value for us, even if our deeds help others (1 Corinthians 13).

There are believers, some of them pastors and leaders, who win unbelievers to the Lord (good deeds), but their own marriages, families, and other relationships are a shambles (lack of love). Or they can give wonderful sermons and teachings but are secretly addicted to pornography or other sexual sins or to substance abuse, or they are violent physically or verbally, or they have ethical lapses in their use of money, or they have other serious sins in their lives. By God's grace they manage to function and do some good in the world, even though their "holiness" is a façade. But their functioning is truly dysfunctional—they are not operating at God's optimal level, and they do damage along with the good they accomplish. Usually the poor quality of their prayer lives and devotional times in the Word of God is an indicator of this sort of difficulty. What is required in such situations is less doing and more being, more receptivity to letting God work in their lives. I call this receiving of God's love being open-heart. Our movement, as well as the church at large, is in drastic need of being more open-heart.

How do we be open-heart? Two requirements are honesty and trust, because only with these can we take down the walls that separate us from our fellows. Six emotions that block the way to being honest and exercising trust are anger, fear, pain, despair, confusion, and shame. Anyone who experiences life dominated by one or more of these negative feelings knows how distressing they are. But others suppress their feelings. They are "in denial," or they dissociate ("space out"), or they cover up. All these make healing more difficult—yet God can heal even these.

The Gentile branch of the body of Messiah has pioneered in this area commonly called inner healing or emotional healing; our movement has lagged behind. This may be due to our fewer numbers, but I think we also have a tendency toward "head orientation" rather than "heart orientation." There is nothing wrong with intellectual clarity. My own lifework has depended on it. Yet the essence of the gospel must touch the heart. No amount of head knowledge can produce or substitute for a genuine change of heart. Among the helpful Christian writers I have encountered are Henry Cloud on emotional boundaries; Paul Meier on codependency; Charles Kraft on deliverance from demonic oppression; Jim Friesen, Jim Wilder, and Larry Crabb on the role of a believing community in healing; Leanne Payne on sexuality and gender roles; Ed Smith on the seminal role that the lies we believe play in the sins we commit; and Jack Frost on father-love. Secular writers can also be helpful, provided we set their truths in a biblical context: for example, Merle Fossum and Marilyn Mason on shame.

The point is that our movement and the individuals comprising it urgently need to face up to the emotional pain and resulting sin from which nearly all of us suffer. Some think it's selfish to seek one's own emotional healing. It isn't, because unhealed believers can't serve God as effectively as they would like. To the degree that believers get healed emotionally they will be able to serve God better, because they will use less energy to suppress pain, fear, anger, shame, confusion, and despair—and thus have more energy available for service.

I predict that this will become a major focus in the Messianic Jewish movement and its congregations, and I especially urge and exhort the leaders to seek emotional and psychological healing for themselves. I also predict that, as we evangelize our own people, among the most effective "signs" Jews ask for (1 Corinthians 1:22) will be the dramatic changes at the psychological and spiritual levels that will result from Messianic Jews getting emotional healing through Yeshua the Messiah. Healed believers are superb witnesses to Yeshua because their transparency and genuineness proclaim his work and his love.

Defining and Pursuing Community

Congregational community grows naturally from emotional healing. A congregation is developing a measure of community if it is a safe place where people can be open and transparent without having to put on a show, if its members are friendly and open with each other and toward outsiders, if they are interested in understanding how others' God-given goals fit into God's larger plan, if they are willing to sacrifice pursuit of their own goals in order to help others attain theirs, if they pray for each other, and if the congregation has goals for itself as a congregation. A congregation in which the main thing members do is sit at meetings that are half music and half sermon is probably not a community, since it will lack the intimacy community implies. I'm sure there are better descriptions of community than mine; all I want to do here is point out that community is a goal to be consciously defined and pursued, for its presence cannot be merely assumed.

Developing a Proper Expression of Jewishness

Messianic Jewish congregations have expended a great deal of energy into developing and refining theological, ceremonial, and practical ways to express Jewishness. This is to be expected, especially in the Diaspora, where Messianic Jews are a double minority—a tiny percentage of Jews and an even tinier percentage of believers in Yeshua. So we find ourselves constantly wanting to prove to Jews that we, too, are Jews, generally by showing that our practices and ceremonies are Jewish in character even though they honor Yeshua, and to Gentile Christians that we, too, believe in Yeshua, generally by showing that our theological positions are sound, even when expressed in Jewish terms.

But this effort spent proving ourselves to others—and to ourselves—distorts our lives, our congregations, and our movement! We should not have the goal of becoming acceptable within the non-Messianic Jewish community—because we never will. Instead, our Jewish practices and ceremonies should be chosen to meet our own needs in expressing our faith, with one eye to what is Jewish and what isn't, and the other eye to what is biblical and what is anti-biblical. (Some things are neither required nor prohibited, but permitted.) If we do this, our congregations will be comfortable places for us to express our faith, both the Jewish and the Messianic aspects, and also places where interested non-Messianic Jews can feel comfortable as they experience what it means to be Messianic.

In the last fifteen years the movement and its congregations have developed Messianic Jewish ceremonial and liturgical aspects of *Shabbat* and the biblical festivals. But in many cases the ceremonies and liturgies have settled into a rut and become ritualized, automatic, and boring. People recite the prayers in rote fashion, as a matter of duty. This is legalism! Often the leaders aren't sure what they can do to solve the problem. My solution is to let the Holy Spirit do his work. When the Holy Spirit is absent, Messianic Jewish liturgies, ceremonies, and customs are performed in the letter and not in the Spirit, so that they bring death instead of life. I have not the slightest doubt that most of the prayers in the Jewish prayer books (the *siddur* and the *machzorim*) can be prayed with joy and wholeheartedness when the people praying are filled with spiritual life by the Holy Spirit emanating from the Father and the Son. The Holy Spirit will show when to use different prayers, and when to stop reciting the traditional ones and begin praying spontaneously. Focus on God, not the liturgy, and let the Holy Spirit guide experimentation and adventure.

While examining how the congregations express Jewishness, I would like to explain what I consider the proper place of the Oral Torah in Messianic Judaism, because this is still a matter of controversy in the movement. To start with, however, I should say that I regard the New Testament as Written Torah. It modifies and adds to the Written Torah that existed prior to Yeshua's coming. I have discussed this and other aspects of how the Torah applies today in chapter 5 of *Messianic Jewish Manifesto*.

I compare the Written Torah with the American constitution. The constitution does not tell in detail how to run the country, but it does set up the legislative, executive, and judicial branches of the government, along with the limits they must observe. Likewise, the Written Torah is inadequate for governing the Jewish nation under all circumstances, but in Deuteronomy 17:8–13 it establishes a method for determining God's will in situations not specifically foreseen in the Written Torah. Cases are to be brought before the court at the city gate, and difficult ones are to be referred to the *cohanim* (priests) and the *shofet* (judge) in office at the time; they are to declare what the Torah requires.

I think this was meant to be a flexible system, allowing two similar cases to yield different verdicts if times changed. Precedents would be noted but could be overridden. The rabbis' takeover of the role of the *cohanim* and *shofet* is not biblically sanctioned, but in this discussion I won't dispute their usurpation of authority. The problem we are left with is that ossification set in as the precedents of the Oral Torah came to be regarded as decreed by God for all time and just as binding as the Written Torah. The U.S. Congress can pass any law that doesn't violate the constitution, and it can decide later to revoke all or part of it. But the Oral Torah has come to be "set in stone" so that its decisions cannot be revoked. The Jewish system of *Halakhah* (law) has had to devise ways to get around previous decisions without revoking them, and sometimes it seems unable to do so. If the Oral Torah, that is, the system for determining how to apply the Written Torah in real life, were as flexible as it is meant to be, it could work. If its rulings had been easier to change, Yeshua might not have had to scold the scribes and the Pharisees, "With your tradition you nullify the word of God" (Mark 7:13).

The reason I am devoting space to this subject is that there are Messianic Jews who reject everything added to the Written Torah by the rabbis as unbiblical. They believe that by doing so they will arrive at truly biblical Judaism. I believe this approach fails. Because the Written Torah does not completely specify the behavior God wants, it still has to be applied. Therefore such a supposedly "biblical Judaism" will end up inventing its own Oral Torah. (The Roman Catholic Church with its canon law and numerous Protestant denominations with their various rules and regulations do precisely this.) There's nothing wrong with it, but it doesn't mean that they have thereby created "biblical Judaism." I believe that the right way to relate to the existing Oral Torah is not as divine command but as religious and cultural tradition, much of which can guide us toward holiness and toward making congregational life both satisfying for ourselves and useful for showing non-Messianic Jews the gospel in the context of who and what we are. Also, relating to the Oral Torah will better prepare us to dialogue with the Jewish religious world if the opportunity arises.

Engaging in Evangelism

Let me say at the outset that evangelism is not an option but a command. A believer who doesn't communicate the gospel to unbelievers is not only sinning against love of his fellow human being by withholding the means of eternal life but is also refusing to obey Yeshua's order to go into all the world and make disciples. Moreover, doing evangelism is one of God's ways of blessing a believer—the reward is the act itself.

Moreover, a congregation cannot be healthy if it is not evangelizing. Just as the human body, in order to be healthy, must interact with the outside world so that, through breathing and eating, it makes some of its environment a part of itself, so a congregation must act to make some of the people outside part of itself. Para-congregrational organizations such as Jews for Jesus and Chosen People Ministries do a praiseworthy job of evangelizing Jewish people, but the normal way for the body of Messiah to grow is to have members of congregations share the life of Yeshua, which they themselves are living, with the people around them.

In Israel I detect a new and exciting phenomenon, one that will bring our movement great joy and vitality. The time has arrived when Orthodox Jews in Israel will begin coming to faith in Yeshua and getting saved. How will this come about—and how has it begun to come about already? Through our speaking to their hearts. For two hundred years it has been taught that to win Jews to Yeshua one must prove that Yeshua fulfills the Messianic prophecies found in the Old Testament and denigrate rabbinic Judaism as a human creation not from God. This has been thought to be the best way to convince Orthodox Jews, traditional Jews, Jewishly educated Jews, to believe in Yeshua. It is not. The song that was a Hit Parade winner in 1945 made this observation:

You gotta ac–cent–tchu–ate the positive,
E–lim–i–nate the negative,
And latch on to the affirmative;
Don't mess with Mister In-Between.

The *positive* that all people need, and at some level want, is a genuine heart-connection with God. They want to receive his love, and they want their sins forgiven—even if they don't know it! They receive this message through us, and the way we transmit it is to have his love to give (which requires emotional healing). Eliminate *negative* attitudes toward "rabbinism." The fact is that rabbinic Judaism, even without Yeshua, has preserved a wealth of godly truth, especially in the area of ethics. Rather than deprecate religious Judaism, assume that an Orthodox Jew is not disenchanted with his tradition but that he still has not found in it what his soul seeks. Thus, being *affirmative* about his lifestyle and negative about nothing, we show that Yeshua can supply his need. To be sure, there are strangenesses in religious Judaism—as there are in every religion, including Christianity and Messianic Judaism. If this weren't true, none of us would ever feel embarrassed about presenting the gospel in a Messianic Jewish way. But most of us do, at one time or another, because we recognize how imperfect we and our congregations are. Yeshua is perfect, but we are *in-between*—clay vessels (2 Corinthians 4:7), and most of us are *broken* clay vessels. So our strategy must be not to pretend we're perfect, but to admit that in us, that is, in our flesh, dwells no good thing (Romans 7:18), and that to the extent that there is anything good about us at all, it is due to God's grace, not our own accomplishment (Ephesians 2:8–10).

I have found it helpful in explaining the gospel to Orthodox Jews to point out that the main topic of the Torah is the sacrificial system, and that the reason is that the punishment for sin is death (Genesis 2:16–17). Thus the Torah introduces vicarious atonement in the form of animal sacrifices. But without a temple there are no sacrifices today, so how can sin be atoned for in modern Judaism? The rabbinic substitution of "repentance, prayer, and charity"[3] for the biblical sacrifices is not authorized by God, and the Orthodox will acknowledge this. In this context

[3]See the *unetaneh tokef* prayer in the *machzor* for the high holidays.

Yeshua the Messiah's atoning sacrificial death on the execution-stake will make sense, and its effectiveness can be understood and received. In this context the Messianic prophecies play an important supporting role.

I foresee that some Orthodox Jews who come to Messianic faith will maintain an Orthodox Jewish lifestyle, while others will veer away from it. No matter what they do, Israeli Orthodox Jews who come to faith will bring exciting new elements to our movement and will have a powerful evangelistic influence on the entire Jewish world, and ultimately on all the nations.

Already Messianic Jews are going out to nations around the world with the gospel, following the examples of Isidor Loewenthal (1826–64), who evangelized in Afghanistan, and Samuel Schereschewsky (1831–1906), who evangelized in China. Since the Iron Curtain fell in Eastern Europe (1989) and the Soviet Union (1991), Messianic Jews such as Jonathan Bernis, Richard Glickstein, and Jeff Bernstein, as well as Jews for Jesus, have discovered an unprecedented degree of openness to the gospel among the Jews in these countries. This is in reaction to the suppression of faith for over seventy years under the Communists. Thousands have come to faith, and Jews who have emigrated from these countries to the West are equally receptive; and we have seen a major move among immigrants to Israel from the former Soviet Union. Messianic Jews who want to recapture the pioneering spirit should seize some of these opportunities.

In addition to evangelism there is pre-evangelism—preparing the emotional, mental, and social ground for the gospel. In this connection my friend Joseph Shulam here in Jerusalem has coined a phrase I like. In Hebrew: *Anachnu tzrikheem lehavee et Yeshua habaitah.* In English: "We need to bring Yeshua back home," back to his own family and people. After two thousand years of being a wandering Jew rejected by the Jewish people and accepted by Gentiles, the image everyone has is of Yeshua having become Gentilized. I'm not referring so much to how he is portrayed in paintings as to how he is described, imagined, understood, and even theologized about by Jews and Christians alike. In consequence, his reality, character, teachings, and lifework are misrepresented. Nearly everyone acknowledges the fact that he was a Jew (an exception: Yasser Arafat, who called him a "great Palestinian"), but few have explored what that really means. We—Joe Shulam and I, and others—think it is high time to bring Yeshua back home where he belongs, where Jewish people can see him as a fellow Jew able to meet the need of every Jewish heart. This process has begun, but it still requires much historical and theological work, and it is one of the tasks the Messianic Jewish movement should pursue diligently.

Preparing for the Land of Israel to Become the Center of Messianic Judaism

The center of the Jewish world shifted from Europe to Israel when the state of Israel was created in 1948. But the world center of Messianic Judaism has remained the United States. Nevertheless I believe that God's promise, "All Israel shall be saved" (Romans 11:26), will increasingly find fulfillment in *Eretz-Israel*, the land of Israel. One reason is simply demographic. In 1948 only 6 percent of world Jewry lived here, whereas now 37 percent do, and the percentage is growing annually. A more fundamental reason is that Israelis rarely have a problem with their Jewish identity because they don't have to define it in relation to a non-Jewish majority. In other words, being and feeling Jewish in Israel is the norm, not the exception. It does not depend on doing Jewish religious things or on consciously developing Jewish culture. In the Diaspora, emphasizing Jewish identity in evangelism diverts attention from Yeshua to Jewishness. Until now most believers have found it hard to reach Israelis with the gospel because many of them were not born and raised in Israel and had to adapt to Jewish Israeli society as outsiders, as immigrants. But now we have raised a generation of believers born in Israel; and they know the Israeli mind-set through and through because it is their own mind-set. These are the ones who will revolutionize Israeli society with the gospel. This is just beginning—a few raindrops—but I predict that it will become a flood! Moreover, when this happens, it will revolutionize the Messianic Jewish movement. I can't tell you how, but it will.

I urge the Messianic Jews of the Diaspora to prepare for Israel's becoming the center of Messianic Judaism by visiting Israel and, at least in some cases, by making *aliyah* (immigrating to Israel), thus becoming part of the process. Yes, it is still possible to make *aliyah,* even after the Beresford decision of 1989 in which Israel's High Court of Justice ruled that Messianic Jews are not eligible to do so under the Israel's Law of Return. (The Law of Return states that every Jew "who has not changed his religion" can become a citizen of Israel; the Beresford decision says that for purposes of the Law of Return Messianic Jews have "changed their religion.") However, you must be careful how you go about it, because you only have one chance to do things right the first time.

Refining Our Theology So As to Help End the Schism between the Body of Messiah and the Jewish People

I have always felt that the major task of Messianic Jews within the body of Messiah is to help heal the greatest schism in history, the breach between the church and the Jewish people. I think the best way to do this is to help Gentile Christians feel comfortable thinking of the Jews as their own people—as "us" not "them"—because that is what Scripture teaches. This requires developing an appropriate ecclesiology.

Ecclesiology is the branch of theology that deals with who constitute God's people and what their role is in God's plan for the human race. Both before Yeshua came and in non-Messianic Judaism today, ecclesiology (although Judaism does not use this term) was simple: The Jews are the people of God, period. After Yeshua it became clear to believers in him that Gentiles who believed in him had joined God's people. Take note: the operative word in this sentence is "joined," not "replaced." For in Ephesians 2:11–13 Paul writes this to non-Jewish Christians:

> Remember your former state: you Gentiles by birth ... at that time had no Messiah. You were estranged from the national life of Israel. You were foreigners to the covenants embodying God's promise. You were in this world without hope and without God. But now, you who were once far off have been brought near through the shedding of the Messiah's blood.

Before having faith in Yeshua the Jewish Messiah, Gentiles were "estranged from the national life of Israel"; but now, as believers, through all that Yeshua did (encapsulated in the phrase "shedding of the Messiah's blood"), they have been "brought near" to the national life of Israel. The term "brought near" doesn't mean "brought close but still outside"; rather, it means "brought all the way into the national life of Israel." This is clear from the following verse (Ephesians 2:14), which states that Yeshua "himself is our *shalom*—he has made us both one and has broken down the *m'chitzah* [wall of separation] which divided us."

But the church, reacting to Jewish nonacceptance of the gospel, instead of thinking of themselves as having joined the national life of Israel and thus accepting with open arms what Jewish believers had provided from their own rich background, developed a "replacement theology," in which the church replaces the Jews as God's people, and God's promises to the Jews are canceled. This theology held sway without significant competition from the fourth century on, and it is still dominant in Christendom today. Protestants developed several less anti-Jewish forms of ecclesiology; yet none of them give any significance to the current activity of the Jewish people. Dispensationalism, for example, says that God is indeed "not finished with the Jews," but he will not significantly begin dealing with them again until "Daniel's seventieth week," which will not come until the church is "raptured" (suddenly removed from the earth and taken to heaven).

We should develop an ecclesiology that takes into account three groups of people corresponding to the olive tree analogy of Romans 11:17–26: the cut-off natural branches grafted back into their own cultivated olive tree (Messianic Jews), the branches of the wild olive tree grafted into the cultivated tree (Gentile Christians), and the cut-off natural branches that have not yet been grafted back in (non-Messianic Jews). What does the olive tree teach us about these three groups of people in relation to the body of Messiah? What impact does this have on relationships—both theologically and practically—between Gentile believers, Jewish believers, and the rest of the Jewish people? What is the current role of Gentile believers, Messianic Jews, and non-Messianic Jews in God's plan? Messianic Jews should be at the forefront of developing further these aspects of theology for the sake of healing the breach between the body of Messiah and the Jewish people, with the result that in the end "all Israel will be saved" (Romans 11:26).

OTHER THINGS

I expect our infrastructure and our culture to grow in size, quality, and depth. There will be more, larger, and better congregations and schools; more and better discipleship; more development of the arts; and more involvement in social and political issues, such as opposing abortion and homosexuality, enhancing the role of women, supporting Israel, fighting anti-Semitism, relieving persecution of Christians, helping the poor, protecting the environment, and in general participating in the overall political life of the countries we live in. All these things continue trends already observed in our movement during the last forty years.

I expect continued progress in developing Messianic Jewish theology, and not only in the areas of ecclesiology and Torah. We will express with increasing clarity our theology of what Christians mean when they talk about the "Trinity" and the "deity of Jesus." And we will explore more deeply and practically the relationship between heart and head and the relationship between sinning and having been emotionally wounded. One area of theology we can take pride in is apologetics: Michael Brown's four-volume *Answering Jewish Objections to Jesus*,[4] which offers a systematic Messianic Jewish approach to this subject, is one of the most exciting and useful products our movement has produced.

Finally, here are some things I hope for:

- a systematic theology book in Hebrew (preferably a Messianic Jewish one, but *any* will do)
- counseling centers in Israel to help Messianic Jews work through personal issues and deal with pain and other negative emotions
- increased *aliyah* (immigration of Jews to Israel)
- increased contact and genuine love between Israeli Jewish believers and Arab Christians, thus demonstrating the gospel in action
- continued progress in reaching out with the gospel to a broad spectrum of the Jewish public—secular, Orthodox, intellectuals, "establishment" people, Jews drawn to the

[4]Michael Brown, *Answering Jewish Objections*, vols. 1–3 (Grand Rapids: Baker, 2000–2003).

New Age movement, and the many other subgroups in the Jewish community

- increased efforts within the Messianic Jewish movement to deal with the Holocaust—for this is still an open wound for our people, and we must walk through this issue with them; if we fail to do so, our message will be truncated and less real

As I edit what I have written, the war between Israel and the Palestinians has entered its thirty-third month. Hundreds on both sides have been killed. The West, under Muslim pressure, has increasingly united against Israel. I see Satan at work behind the scenes, as we move toward Zechariah 12, when the whole world comes against Jerusalem. But with our message of salvation for everyone, Jew and Gentile alike, we were born "for such a time as this" (Esther 4:14). As Messianic Jews, let us connect intimately with our God, be true disciples who can transmit his love through Yeshua to others, and rise to the challenge of doing the works God has prepared for us to do (Ephesians 2:10) in these momentous days.

APPENDIX: MESSIANIC MOVEMENT ORGANIZATIONS

The following is not an endorsement from the editor, contributors, or publisher. It merely provides a representative listing of organizations for readers who want to do further research or to locate Messianic congregations in their local areas.

Ariel Ministries
P.O. Box 3723, Tustin, CA 92781
Phone: 714-259-4800
Fax: 714-259-1092
E-mail: HomeOffice@ariel.org
Internet: http://www.ariel.org

Chosen People Ministries
International Headquarters:
241 East 51st Street, New York, NY 10022
Phone: 212-223-2252
In Canada: P.O. Box 897
Sta. B–North York, ON M2K 2R1
Phone: 416-250-0177
Internet: http://www.chosen-people.com

International Alliance of Messianic
Congregations and Synagogues
P.O. Box 20006, Sarasota, FL 34276-3006
Phone: 866-426-2766
E-mail: info@iamcs.org
Internet: http://iamcs.org

International Federation of Messianic Jews
P.O. Box 271708, Tampa, FL 33688

Phone: 813-920-0864
E-mail: webmaster@ifmj.org
Internet: http://www.ifmj.org

International Messianic Jewish Alliance
P.O. Box 6307, Virginia Beach, VA 23456
Phone: 757-495-8246
Fax: 757-495-8276
E-mail: Shalom@imja.com or Office@imja.com
Internet: http://www.imja.org

Jews for Jesus
International Headquarters: 60 Haight Street
San Francisco, CA 94102
Phone: 415-864-2600
Fax: 415-552-8325
E-mail: jfj@jewsforjesus.org
Internet: http://www.jewsforjesus.org

Menorah Ministries
P.O. Box 460024, Glendale, CO 80246-0024
Phone: 303-355-2009
Fax: 303-355-6901
E-mail: menorah@menorah.org
Internet: http://www.menorah.org

Menorah Ministries (Rabbi Dr. John Fischer's
Messianic Jewish international ministry)
P.O. Box 669, Palm Harbor, FL 34682
Phone: 727-726-1472
Fax: 727-724-6090
E-mail: BetMidrash@aol.com
Internet: http://www.menorahministries.com

Messianic Jewish Alliance of America
P.O. Box 274, Springfield, PA 19064
Phone: 800-225-MJAA (6522)
Fax: 610-338-0471
E-mail: http://info@mjaa.org
Internet: http://www.mjaa.org

Messianic Jewish Movement International
P.O. Box 1212, Chandler, AZ 85244-1212
Phone: 800-4YESHUA (493-7482)
Phone/Fax: 480-786-MJMI (6564)
E-mail: office@mjmi.org
Internet: http://www.mjmi.org

Union of Messianic Jewish Congregations
529 Jefferson St. NE, Albuquerque, NM 87108
Phone: 800-692-UMJC (8652)
E-mail: office@umjc.org
Internet: http://www.umjc.org

SCRIPTURE INDEX

SUBJECT INDEX

Printed in the USA
CPSIA information can be obtained
at www.ICGtesting.com
JSHW032116191223
54022JS00004B/9